cooking

under the influence

Dedication

To Margaret Fulton, Scotland's greatest Australian, and Australia's most influential cooking writer. Before all the celebrity chefs, she helped this nation make some sense of its emerging multitudinous foodstuffs. She taught many of us the basics, and also some more complex culinary moves. From shortcrust pastry in the food processor to Finnish Karelian Hotpot...thanks Margaret.

This edition first published in Canada in 2005 by Whitecap Books.
351 Lynne Ave, North Vancouver, British Columbia, Canada, V7J 2C4.
www.whitecap.ca

ISBN 1 55285 698 4

Concept and art direction: Marylouise Brammer
Project manager: Margaret Malone
Photographer: Tim Robinson
Creative consultant and stylist: Marcus Hay
Food styling and food preparation: Ross Dobson
Food editor: Katy Holder
Editor: Kim Rowney
Editorial director: Diana Hill
Production: Monika Paratore
Photographer's assistant: Lauren Trompp
Stylist's assistants: Tamara Boon and Nicolle Churi

Chief executive: Juliet Rogers
Publisher: Kay Scarlett

Printed by 1010 Printing Limited. Printed in China.

IMPORTANT: Those who might be at risk from the effects of salmonella poisoning (the elderly, pregnant women, young children and those suffering from immune deficiency diseases) should consult their doctor with any concerns about eating raw eggs.
NOTE: We have used 20 ml tablespoon measures. If you are using a 15 ml tablespoon, for most recipes the difference will not be noticeable. However, for recipes using small amounts of flour and cornflour (cornstarch), add an extra teaspoon for each tablespoon specified.

The publisher and stylist would like to thank the following for their generosity in supplying furniture, props, antiques and kitchenware: Art of Wine and Food, Bison, David Edmonds, Design Mode International, G.L Auchinachie and Son, Mix(d), Mud Australia, Orson & Blake, Parterre Garden, The Sydney Antique Centre, Waterford Wedgwood, and Wheel & Barrow; Cloth, and Signature Prints for some fabric and wallpaper backgrounds; paint for backgrounds supplied by Porter's Paints; Flash Trash, Funk Me, Mix(d), Newtown Old Wares, and Thonet for furniture.

Special thanks goes to Tamara Boon and family for the use of their home, and Tina and Matthew Ryan of Wild Rhino PR for their hospitality, accommodation and generous use of their property for photography.

cooking

under the influence

food to drink to

ben canaider + greg duncan powell

whitecap

contents

core brand values

Wine and food are natural, easy partners. But somewhere sometime someone seems to have forgotten that. In the world we live in wine writing and food writing are demarcated careers; they're rarely allowed to appear together. When they are, it's under the nouveau-science of food and wine matching, where it is determined which wine you are allowed to drink with which food, and vice versa.

This book sets out to pull that apart, but it also wants to put it loosely back together. After all, we are drinks writers who — as strange as this might sound — eat as well as drink. We've noticed that many of our fellow human beings do the same. Our aim is to bring a little more wine and a little less prescription back into the kitchen. We believe that ingredients are more than the playdough of food stylists or the passionate *raison d'être* of chefs; wine is not a weapon with which to fight your way up society's escalator. The recipes herein are the result of our eating and drinking lives. It's food cooked with an eye — or stomach — more towards flavour than finery, and effect rather than affectation. The wine advice is a guide not a command. If you choose to drink something completely different to what we've suggested, that's OK.

After all, we eat and drink in search of nutrients. We ingest them; we digest them. This rather unromantic version of 'fine dining' and 'wine appreciation' is always worth remembering — just to keep the whole thing in perspective. This book was written with that in mind. More importantly, we've lived on this sort of food and drink for a while now, and we're still going strong…

Ben and Greg

6

this goes with that...
wine for food, and vice versa

Human beings are strange creatures. The longing for freedom is strong, yet even stronger is the urge to restrain that freedom. So we have things like marriage, seatbelts, five-day weeks, and silly dictates on wine and food matching. On that last point, the whole wine and food matching thing has become so ridiculous that in the interests of clarity it's best to restate a few truths.

- Wine is food.

- Consuming wine with other foods is not a new concept.

- Consuming wine that clashes with the food you are eating WILL NOT KILL YOU.

- Some wines go better with some foods than others.

All are important to remember. Wine and food is not a mathematical equation, yet people seem to want to know what is right. They want — as per usual — answers to uncertainties. There are no hard and fast answers, however. Both wine and food are inexact sciences, just like predicting the weather.

If that prospect is too anarchic and you'd prefer something more analytical — even prescriptive — we've developed what we believe to be the simplest and most original way to work out if what you're eating/drinking is going to make what you're drinking/eating taste better or worse. Because that's what it's all about, isn't it?

9

the powell-canaider five senses food and wine matrix

1. sight

Colour and clarity can hint at quality, power and age. Wine judges even give the appearance a score.

a Colour: The most obvious indicator and the oldest rule: white wine = white meat, red wine = red meat. It's the most basic tenet of putting wine with food and mostly it works. A piquant white goes much better with a bit of fish than a young, tannic red. But a bit of barbecued chook definitely prefers the latter. So don't get stuck on it.

b Age: You can tell the age of a wine just by looking at it. Older whites are more yellow or golden; older reds more garnet, and less purple. The actual age in years is not as important as how old the wine tastes. As a general rule, young wines go better with fresher, less cooked food; older wines go better with food that's been cooked to within an inch of its life. Slowly braised beef with old shiraz is a classic example.

2. taste

The mouth registers sweetness, acidity, bitterness and saltiness.

a Sweetness: Nothing can make a wine taste worse than when the food is sweeter than the wine. In putting wines with sweet things, make sure the wine is sweeter than the food or the wine will taste thin and mean. Overkill here is much more effective than underkill.

b Acidity: Crucial to the equation. Everyone has experienced the salad-dressing-makes-the-wine-taste-thin syndrome. To avoid this, the acidity in the wine has to be greater than the acidity in what you're eating. No wine will be improved by eating a raw lemon, but a sharp, acidic white can easily handle — or even take the place of — a squeeze of lemon on a piece of fish.

c Bitterness: While an aggressive young red can seem bitter when drunk on its own, taste it after swallowing a mouthful of seasoned lamb shank and that same red will taste perfectly balanced. Likewise, the lamb shank will seem far less glutinous than it did on its own. It's the magic of fat and tannin at work, one of the world's great synergistic relationships.

d Saltiness: Salt tends to cancel out acidity and bitterness, which means that salt is a great friend to wine. Really salty food goes quite well with highly acidic wines — olive tapenade and sharp bubbly for instance. Likewise, powerful, gruff reds don't seem as aggressive and undrinkable when you're tucking into a kilo of corned beef.

3. touch

Your tongue and mouth register a food or drink's weight, texture and temperature.

a Weight: Where weight or body are concerned, opposites attract. They provide relief. Lightly weighted yet well-structured pinot noir is better with duck than a weighty cabernet, and limpid dry whites are preferable to oily chardonnays when tucking into a fish rich in omega 3s.

b Texture: Texture can tie wine and food together in quite a beautiful knot. The fluffiness of champagne and a pillowy omelette; the unctuousness of liqueur muscat and the silky creaminess of homemade ice cream...

c Temperature: There are some rudiments to observe here: cold food = cold wine. For example, fresh oysters on ice and a heavily chilled dry white. If the meal is hot, don't make the wine too cold or you won't taste a damn thing.

4. smell

Otherwise called olfaction.

a Wine as a condiment: This relies on age-old flavour combinations. A peppery smelling shiraz with a scotch fillet, or a lemony dry white with a piece of fish. It's simple but it works.

b Picking out notes: This is a bit trickier. It involves picking out a nuance in the wine and matching it up with a subtle flavour in the dish. Such as putting a red wine with a hint of liquorice alongside a dish flavoured by star anise, or drinking the bergamot-scented pinot with *canard à l'orange*.

5. sound

Yes, sound can have a gastronomic impact. It works in two ways:

a Auditory: The sound of a fridge door opening and closing followed by a Champagne cork gently hissing out of the bottle's neck; the sound of the oven's fan-forced facility whirring away as the old cork is gently sighed from a bottle of well-cellared cabernet; the tiny click of a riesling bottle's screwcap twisting off as an oyster shucker's blade snaps the adductor muscle on a fresh *crassostrea gigas*; or the crack of a can of beer just seconds before the air-sucking whoosh of a gas-lit barbecue igniting...

b Association: Some combinations just sound wrong. Like the names of couples that you can tell just shouldn't be together. Tamsen and Wayne. Spencer and Jane. Put Wayne with Jane, and Tamsen with Spencer and everyone will be happy ever after. Food and wine are the same. Sausages and Champagne. Cabernet and canapés. Reversing them is obvious, but it's surprising how many of us trip up on this very elemental stuff.

weeknight

whip-ups

weeknight whip-ups

'And to Adam he said,
   Because you have listened to the voice of your
   wife, and you have eaten of the tree of which I
   commanded you,
   You shall not eat of it, cursed is the ground because
   of you; in toil you shall eat of it all the days of your
   life; thorns and thistles it shall bring forth to you;
   and you shall eat the plants of the field.
   In the sweat of your face you shall eat bread till
   you return to the ground, for out of it you were
   taken; you are dust, and to dust you shall return.'

The Old Testament, Genesis 2:17

It could have been another way, but because Eve was sucked in by that snake to take a nibble on the fruit of the tree of knowledge — otherwise known as a Royal Gala — we have a five-day working week, eight-hour days and workplace agreements. You're not working to buy that house/car/CD/caffe latte; you're working because of something that happened a long time ago. For Eve's sin, Man is condemned to toil, to labour, and to live on frozen food. As the graffiti along the train line reads: 'Work. Eat. Shit. Die.' That's Genesis 2:17, version twenty-first century.

But the Lord is a merciful God and he has given us the blessings — indeed, the miracles — of wine and those few precious hours at home on weeknights. It's your chance to get in the kitchen and get back to the Garden.

Rather than understanding that home is a sanctuary, we often see it as a kind of purgatory — we get home and go into a holding pattern before hitting the work tarmac at 8 a.m. the next day. It's too expensive to go out; I'll miss my favourite telly show; I've got work tomorrow — human habitats become facilities for self-imposed house arrest. If you're pessimistic enough to count them, there are plenty of reasons for *not* cooking. You're tired, the kitchen gets dirty, cooking creates smells, ingredients make mess, pots and pans need washing up, the knives are blunt, you might cut yourself (if they were sharp), there's that sitcom on telly they'll all be talking about at work tomorrow...

But take a look at it from the other side. This is your chance to salvage something of your day — an opportunity to create something for yourself when all day you've been doing everything for everyone else. It's a chance to change the nature of your house/flat/caravan; to fill it with exotic aromas; to cook and to dream. In these few precious hours your brain gets a chance to relax — just like resting a joint of roasted meat. In both meat and brain, the juices concentrate. The resultant eating and thinking is therefore more pleasurable, more rewarding, more tender... One extra glass of wine and you get a glimpse of the Garden of Eden — until the alarm goes off at 7 a.m.

15

spaghetti alla bere bere

Before 1976 Australians, for the most part, cooked spaghetti for 2 hours and then ladled a bit of tinned bolog-nay-zay on top. It was the sort of food designed to slip off your plate as you carried it to the TV chair. What it did to shagpile carpets should have told us what it could do to our stomachs. We've come a long way, however. Now oddly named pasta — Fusion Fusilli, Pacific Rim Penne — is cooked until al dente and has Thai-inspired coriander pesto and kumera chunks thrown on it. Somewhere between the old spag bol and the new fusion dishes we've missed the real deal. A good, authentic, untrendy sauce — or *sugo*, as Italians like Ben call it — is one of three important keys to a good pasta dish. Cooking good-quality, hard durum wheat pasta to al dente is the second, then properly combining the *sugo* and pasta, the third. Alla Bere Bere is named for an old friend who knew how important it was to observe these three steps.

buying

olive oil
4 rashers of bacon, rind removed, cut into thin strips
4 x 1 cm (1/2 inch) thick slices of mild pancetta, cut into
    thin strips
1 onion
1 garlic clove, finely chopped
2 x 400 g (14 oz) tins of whole Roma (plum) tomatoes,
    roughly chopped
500 g (1 lb 2 oz) spaghetti
1 tablespoon pesto
1 heaped teaspoon unsalted butter
grated Parmigiano Reggiano cheese, to serve

17

cooking

Put a big stainless-steel frying pan (one that has a lid) over medium heat. Add a tablespoon of olive oil to the pan and add the bacon and pancetta. Cook them until the base of the pan has coloured a little. While the pan is doing this, finely chop the onion. Add it to the pan, bringing the heat up to high. Stir more than occasionally, adjusting the heat if the onion starts to burn. After 5 minutes, add the garlic and, immediately thereafter, the tomatoes.

Bring this sauce to the boil, pop the lid on (slightly ajar) and lower the heat to a low simmer. Cook for a minimum of 40 minutes, stirring occasionally. The longer and slower the cooking, the better the result.

Cook your pasta. When it is just about al dente, stir the pesto and butter into the tomato sauce. Drain the pasta and add it to the frying pan with the sauce. Mix it all about over a low heat. If the mixture is too dry, add a spot of water. Serve onto warm plates or bowls. Grated Parmigiano is essential. Serves 4

drinking

Because of the texture of this sauce — the meatiness of the bacon, the acidity of the tomatoes, the sweetness of the onion and the nutty, herbal earthiness of the pesto — you need red wine with an earthy, open texture. Grenache that is not too fruity can do the trick, as can a similarly rustic shiraz. Sangiovese can come into its own here too — cheap imports and better Australian versions. Savoury flavours are needed with this dish.

tips+tricks+tabletalk

Add one anchovy fillet to the sauce at the same time as you add the garlic. This will add even more complexity and depth to the *sugo*.

Substitute hot pancetta for the mild pancetta for a bit more chilli oomph — not a bad idea if the wine you've got is a bit rough or rugged.

Spaghettini can replace the slightly thicker spaghetti, if preferred. Oh, and never serve this to Her Majesty Queen Elizabeth II. Royal dining protocol forbids the serving of spaghetti to HM when she's on tour — potentially too messy.

spaghetti alla bere bere

succulent breasts

succulent breasts

Chicken breasts can be as dry and boring as they are commonplace. This recipe, however, guarantees juicy white breast meat that is succulent and tender and will satisfy hard-core carnivores. Such densely textured muscle tissue, as you find in chicken breast, needs wine to help ingesting and digesting. That's wine's job, after all.

20

buying

4 chicken breasts, skin on
1 heaped tablespoon plain (all-purpose) flour
2 teaspoons olive oil
3 teaspoons butter
juice of 1/2 lemon
a dash of dry white wine — whatever you're drinking
250 ml (1 cup) chicken stock
a sprig of lemon thyme, if you've got it
freshly ground black pepper

cooking

The aim for this dish is to get the chicken nicely browned and establish a good brown base on the frying pan — that's for the sauce (a non-stick pan is no good for this recipe). The heat needs to be not so hot that it burns, and not so low that it stews.

First, preheat the oven to 100°C (200°F/Gas 1/2). Dust the chicken breast with the flour. Put a stainless-steel frying pan (one with a lid) over high heat and once it's got some decent heat in it, add the olive oil and 2 teaspoons of the butter. Quickly swill this around the pan and then add the chicken breasts, skin-side down. Reduce the heat to medium and cover with the lid, slightly ajar.

Cook on that side for 7 minutes or so, then turn the breasts over, replace the lid and turn the heat to low. Cook for another 10 minutes. If the pan starts to blacken, throw in 1 or 2 tablespoons of white wine or water. The cooking time of the chicken — and therefore its succulence — is going to depend on the following three things: the size of the chicken breast, the heat of your stove, and the type of pan. Practise. Once cooked, place the chicken on a warm plate in the warm oven.

Turn the heat below the frying pan back to high and pour on the lemon juice, the white wine (beware of flames), the stock and the thyme, if using. Scrape the bottom of the pan with a flat wooden spoon to remove all the browned bits. Simmer until the sauce has reduced in volume by two-thirds. Turn off the heat and add the remaining teaspoon of butter to the sauce, swirling it around the pan until it is melted into the sauce.

Plate. Chicken. Sauce. Salt. Pepper. Serve with green vegetables and a starch of your choice. Serves 4

drinking

This dish is densely fleshed but doesn't have a lot of chicken flavour — it's a vehicle for the sauce, so forget the white-wine-with-white-flesh rule for a start. This is chicken for red wine. Those burnt flavours in the pan and the density of the chicken breast mean you need a red with structure. No invertebrates please. Try cool-climate shiraz with very little oak influence, possibly a cheap Chianti from Italy, or try an affordable Côtes du Rhône red.

tips+tricks+tabletalk

Only season the chicken once plated. You don't want burnt cracked pepper flavours and you don't want the salt to suck the juice out of the meat. Remember, this is all about succulence.

Simple, quick and also satisfying, here's a curry that almost makes itself — and is not so overpowering that it becomes indigestible (you know how some curries can be). Its only problem: it can be slightly addictive.

buying

1 tablespoon olive oil
8 skinless chicken thigh fillets
1–1 1/2 tablespoons Thai green curry paste
2 peeled waxy potatoes (250 g/9 oz), chopped into rough cubes
the same amount of peeled pumpkin, chopped into rough cubes (Kent or Jap is best; avoid Queensland blue or butternut pumpkin/squash)
1–2 chillies, deseeded and roughly chopped
250 ml (1 cup) chicken stock or water
300 ml (10 1/2 fl oz) coconut milk

cooking

Put a big stainless-steel saucepan over high heat, add the olive oil and give it 30 seconds to heat up. Add the chicken in whole pieces. Reduce the heat to medium and brown the chicken on one side for 5 minutes. Add the green curry paste and flip the chicken, then add the potato and pumpkin. Throw in the chilli, stir everything about, then pour on the stock. Pop the lid on and cook over a low heat for 20 minutes.

Remove the lid, add the coconut milk, stir it about again, and cook uncovered for another 5–10 minutes, until the sauce has reached a slightly gluey consistency. Serve with jasmine or basmati rice and a simple green salad with cucumber mixed through it. Serves 4

drinking

The heat of the curry, although not strong enough to blow your doors off, won't do your poncy, complex wines any favours. This food is tailor-made for a fruity, berried cask red wine — try a shiraz. Or if you want to try white, we'd recommend something fairly oily and not too powerfully flavoured — maybe one of those cheap West Australian white blends.

25 Kingfish is one of those fish that fishmongers used to despise, and so was priced accordingly. But sadly, it's now becoming trendy... It's got plenty of all those omega 3 fatty acids, which are good for your cholesterol, your asthma and, more traditionally, your Datsun's chassis. Kingfish is best as cutlets and it loves the barbie, but is also good in a pan with olive oil — the crispy, deep-fried crust that the hot pan and oil provide, and the juicy succulent inner layer of the cutlet... With a squeeze of lemon and a glass of white wine, you couldn't want for anything else.

kingfish in olive oil

Use garlic in this dish to make it go with lighter reds, such as cheap shiraz and merlot. Paste the garlic clove (see tips, page 35) and throw it around in the pan towards the very, very end of the cooking process. tips+tricks+tabletalk

When buying fish cutlets, try to choose the whole, rounder ones taken from the tail end, not the cutlets from around the stomach cavity. Let someone else buy those. Cavity cutlets normally have more bones, sometimes a stronger gutsy flavour and, in fish like salmon, they're fattier.

buying

60 ml (1/4 cup) olive oil

4 kingfish cutlets (or bonito or mackerel if you absolutely
   can't get kingfish, but don't, whatever you do, use marlin
   or swordfish)

6 tablespoons (1/2 cup) very, very finely chopped flat-leaf
   (Italian) parsley

2 lemons, halved

sea salt and freshly ground black pepper

cooking

Put a non-stick frying pan on the stove. High heat. Add the oil and when it is just about to smoke, slip in the cutlets. Reduce the heat to medium, or medium to high if you've got a lazy stove, and do not frig with the fish. Leave it there until the tops of the cutlets begin to bead with the fish's inner juices — you'll notice this particularly around the centre bone. Then turn it over. You should have a nice crust on the cooked surface. Cook the other side for 2 minutes, or a bit longer if your cutlets are quite thick.

Plonk the fish onto warmed plates and sprinkle over the parsley that you've spent ages chopping up. Squeeze over half a lemon per cutlet, sprinkle with stacks of sea salt, go light on the pepper and serve with chips (see Bundle Hill Chips, page 203). Serves 4

26

drinking

According to Ben, you cannot cook fish unless you're drinking wine. And if you want to drink red wine with fish — easy — drink all the white wine before you cook the fish. The red will then match... eventually. This is a dish that can make really ordinary, thin, acidic whites taste fantastic. So choose young unwooded semillon, marsanne or clean, lean cool-climate chardonnay. Steer clear of floral rieslings, overoaked chardonnay and definitely do not drink verdelho — with anything.

The reason rump is called rump is fairly obvious — it comes from the arse end of the cow.

rump ration

Like all beef cuts, rump has its virtues and its tragic flaws. Whilst it has plenty of true beef flavour, there's hardly any intramuscular fat (cows do a lot of walking as they graze and so their rump is fairly muscly), so while low-fat freaks love it, it can be a bit dry and chewy. But there are cooking techniques that help you to avoid this problem. The whole lack-of-fat thing can be solved by marinating the meat in some olive oil, and tenderness can be encouraged by being very careful when cooking it — cook the steak in one piece and let it rest for a few minutes before serving it.

buying

a sprig of rosemary
a sprig of oregano
a sprig of sage
a handful of parsley
2 tablespoons olive oil
1 kg (2 lb 4 oz) rump steak
1 lemon, cut into wedges

31

cooking

You'll need a barbecue. Turn the grill to high and let it warm up for a good 10 minutes. Whilst waiting for it to warm up, whizz the herbs, olive oil and a little bit of salt and pepper in a food processor, or pound everything together using a mortar and pestle until you've formed a very rough paste. Apply this to the surface of the steaks, making sure they are coated evenly. If you've got time, leave them to marinate for an hour or so in the fridge.

Drop the meat onto the barbecue grill. Cook until the meat's juices appear on the top side. This can take anywhere from 4 minutes to forever, depending on the thickness of the meat and the heat of the barbie. (It's better to cook meat by this method — waiting for the juices to bead — than it is by following arbitrary units of time.)

Once the beading has happened, turn the meat and cook for half the time it's taken you to cook the first side. Turn off the barbie — and the gas at the tap — move the rump to a cooler part of the barbecue and leave it there for 5 minutes to relax. Depending on the size of the steak or steaks, divide into four portions, making sure that the two different muscles that comprise the rump steak are equally distributed. Serve with wedges of lemon, and potato salad (see Salade de Spud, page 217) or chips (see Bundle Hill Chips, page 203). Serves 4

drinking

As we said, there's not a lot of fat in rump steak. It is a lean, densely textured meat and that fatlessness means it can't counter the tannin in a big, gruff wine. So steer clear of young agro cabernets. Instead, choose savoury shiraz, from cooler climes — wines that rely on acid for their structure rather than tannin. The acid helps cut through all that dense muscle. The added bonus in a cool-climate shiraz is that they're peppery — you've then got the wine and the condiment in one.

tips+tricks+tabletalk

Traditional rump steak is a cross-section of two muscles. In supermarkets this doesn't often appear to be the case: the rump can be chopped up into smaller portions and it's hard to tell which bit you're getting — the good bit or the bad bit. Even if you've got no money, it's worth going to a butcher and buying one big, long, traditionally cut piece of rump. You're then in control.

This is a dish better executed on a barbecue grill rather than a hotplate — a hotplate is really just like having a frying pan outside.

This amazingly sustaining and healthful soup is a bit like gruel for grown-ups. Gruel, of course, was a thin oatmeal porridge with a few dead vegetables and some dodgy meat thrown in — if you were lucky. Gruel kept the Medievals going. This more robust and generous version will do the same for you.

pearl barley and ham hock

60 ml (1/4 cup) olive oil
1/2 onion, finely chopped
1/2 carrot, ditto
1 celery stalk, ditto
any other dead vegetables you find in the bottom of the fridge, such as broccoli, beans, peas — finely chop them and throw them in (avoid pumpkin, potato or eggplant/aubergine)
1 small ham hock — ask the butcher to saw this into a few pieces for you
375 g (13 oz) pearl barley, or any packet of soup mix with a high pearl barley component
grated Parmigiano Reggiano or Cheddar cheese (optional)

buying

33

cooking

Put a big heavy-based saucepan or flameproof casserole dish onto the stove. Medium heat. Add the oil and, when hot, add the vegetables. Sauté them for 5 minutes, or until they are softened. Add the hock, the barley and top up the pan with water, covering the solids by at least 5 cm (2 inches). Bring this to the boil, then immediately turn down the heat to very, very, nearly-going-out low.

Put the lid on, ajar, and cook for as long as it takes. You want the ham to easily pull away from the bone, and the soup to take on a thick, gruelly texture. If at any stage the pan dries out too much, top up with some water, 125 ml (1/2 cup) at a time. 2 hours of slow cooking should do it. Remove the ham bone, cool slightly, then tear the meat off the bone, roughly chop it and return the meat to the soup. Reheat if necessary. Grated cheese adds to the bucolic satisfaction. Serves 4

drinking

A glass of dry, neutral white wine, like Soave from Italy or marsanne from France or Australia, is good. Or get stuck into some lean shiraz — the pepper and earth flavours so typical of this wine love this soupy, stewy concoction. Rhône blends — grenache, shiraz and mataro — are similarly like-minded. If it's a really cold night and you've selfishly assigned yourself a fair bit of the ham hock, try some durif.

spiced salmon

Salmon is so boring that it needs all the help it can get. And when your day at work has sucked you dry of energy and imagination, it is also the perfect vehicle for a slightly muted weeknight imagination — and slightly muted weeknight drinking.

buying

4 thick salmon cutlets, tail-end ones
1 heaped teaspoon ground cumin
ditto ground coriander
ditto ground turmeric
1 teaspoon olive oil
1/2 lemon or lime

cooking

Put four dinner plates in a low oven to warm. Put the salmon and ground spices into a thick plastic bag and shake it all around, making sure the surfaces of all the cutlets are well coated with the spices.

Heat the barbecue hotplate or large non-stick frying pan to high. Drop the olive oil onto the hot hotplate or into the pan, add the cutlets (if your cutlets are of uneven size, delay the addition of the thinner cutlets to the hotplate by 1 minute) and cook on one side for 4–5 minutes, depending on the thickness of the fish. Turn. Medium heat. Cook for another 5 minutes. Take them off the heat when there is still a generous seam of raw salmon through the middle of the cutlet. This might look scary but the salmon will continue to cook on the heated plates.

Serve immediately on warmed plates with couscous (see Coo-coo, page 215). Add a squeeze of lemon or lime to each cutlet. Serves 4

drinking

There are a few things going on here: you've got fat, oily fishiness from the salmon and the fragrant earthiness of the spicy crust. This means that salmon can be a red-wine food. Pinot noir. Your favourite, affordable one.

Fresh coriander (cilantro), finely chopped, could be a good garnish. Or pound it to a paste in a mortar and pestle with the ground spices, then rub it over the salmon before you cook it.

tips+tricks+tabletalk

rocket pasta

If the weeknight is a hot or humid one and
the apartamento is stuffy, this is a very
quick and revitalizing pasta dish — indeed,
it is more of a tonic than a dinner.

buying

sea salt
500 g (1 lb 2 oz) expensive spaghettini, but not the
handmade or fresh stuff
2–3 tablespoons fruity, extra virgin olive oil
1 garlic clove, pasted (see tips)
juice of 1 lemon
2 bunches of rocket (arugula), leaves torn
freshly ground black pepper
a chunk of Parmigiano Reggiano cheese, grated

cooking

Bring a large saucepan of water to a rolling boil, add 1 teaspoon of sea
salt and then the pasta. Make sure you push the pasta around a bit,
using a wooden spoon or pasta stirrer to submerge all the spaghettini.

Put a large frying pan on the stove. Low heat. When the pasta is almost
al dente, add 2 tablespoons of olive oil to the frying pan. Drain the
pasta. Add the garlic to the frying pan and cook for 30 seconds. Turn
the heat to high, add the drained pasta, the lemon juice, the rocket
leaves and four twists of the pepper mill. Reduce the heat to low and
stir everything about until it's well combined. Add a touch more olive oil
to the mixture if it seems too dry.

As with all pasta dishes, the trick is in the final act: combining the
pasta with its sauce. Too dry or too oily and the result is up the spout.
Warm bowls. Grated cheese. A sprinkle of sea salt. Serves 4

drinking

Strident white wine is needed here. You want herbal and
reasonably acidic blanc to match the punching weight
of the key ingredients. Sauvignon blanc that's more mineral
than cat's wee, a semillon-sauvignon blanc blend that is not
too fruity, unwooded chardonnay (someone has to drink it) or
cheap blended whites. Some verdicchio from Italy also works.

tips+tricks+tabletalk

Don't use homemade or fresh pasta for this dish, as the oily sauce demands the chalky texture of al dente factory-made spag.

To paste a garlic clove, put the peeled clove on a chopping board and flatten it with the flat side of a knife. Sprinkle with 1 teaspoon of salt then, using the flat side of the knife, work the salt into the garlic to form a pulp, or paste. Alternatively, do this using a mortar and pestle.

spiced salmon

rocket pasta

mini eggplant lasagnes

If you head for the vegetable drawer of your fridge and rummage around, you're bound to find a couple of eggplants. They'll be old, so they're destined for lasagne.

buying

2 tablespoons extra virgin olive oil
1 garlic clove, pasted (see tips, page 35)
400 g (14 oz) tin of Italian tomatoes
10 sheets of dried lasagne
2 eggplants (aubergines), each cut lengthways into
    10 x 4 mm (1/4 inch) thick slices
2 heaped teaspoons pesto
1 small tub of bocconcini, each ball cut into thin discs
100 g (3 1/2 oz) Grana Padano cheese or Parmigiano
    Reggiano cheese, grated

cooking

Whip up the sauce first. Into a stainless-steel saucepan (over medium to high heat) throw the oil, garlic and tomatoes. Simmer this in a fairly vigorous manner in order to reduce it to a suitably saucy consistency, stirring occasionally. Cook the dried lasagne sheets as per the instructions on the packet. Drain the sheets and lay them out flat on a wet tea towel so they don't stick to each other.

Get a non-stick frying pan on high heat and, when it is scary-hot, lay the eggplant slices in a single layer and el scorchio them for 1 minute each side. Stir the pesto through the sauce. Preheat the oven to 180°C (350°F/Gas 4).

Now assemble the mini lasagnes. From the ground up: oiled baking tray, eggplant slice, thin layer of sauce, pasta sheet (cut these strips to fit the size of the eggplant slice), a few discs of bocconcini, another eggplant slice... When you've added the second layer of bocconcini, sprinkle some grated cheese over. That's it. Continue in this manner to make ten lasagnes in total. Put the tray in the hot oven and bake for 20 minutes. Then turn off the oven and let them rest in there for 10 minutes before serving. Serve one each as an entrée, or serve two lasagnes per person as a light meal, with a salad.

drinking

Apparently tomatoes ruin good wine. Tell Italy that. Use a dry rather than too-fruity grenache for this dish. Lightweight merlot is good too, as is that cheap, pretty gruff Chianti found in supermarket grog shops. If eating the lasagne as an entrée, use a dry rosé.

stoutly flattered bathead

One evening when making beer batter, and having drunk all his lager, Greg cleverly substituted a bottle of stout. The result was fantastic.

buying

800 g–1 kg (1 lb 12 oz–2 lb 4 oz) flathead fillets
125 g (1 cup) plain (all-purpose) flour
1 egg
about 60 ml (1/4 cup) milk
1 stubby (375 ml/1 1/2 cups) of good stout, such as Coopers or Southwark
vegetable or olive oil, for deep-frying
lemon wedges, to serve

cooking

First prepare the flathead. If the rib bits and little side fins are still attached, cut them off. Remove the skin using a sharp, thin knife. Lay the fish skin-side down on the chopping board and, working from the tail upwards, separate the skin from the flesh. It's easier than it sounds.

To make the beer batter, mix the flour, egg and milk in a bowl, adding enough milk to make a thick paste. Give it a good whisk. Set the batter aside. Drink half of the stubby of stout.

Half-fill a deep-fat fryer, saucepan or wok (make sure the wok is stable) with oil and heat to 190°C (375°F), or until a cube of bread dropped into the oil browns in 10 seconds. By now the batter will have thickened. Now, gradually add the remaining half stubby of stout to the batter. You want quite a runny batter — fish with a batter skin, not a batter overcoat.

Stir the batter, dip in your fish pieces, then remove and allow any excess batter to drip off. Place the fish gently in the oil, a few at a time. Don't overcrowd the fish in the oil or the temperature of the oil will fall and they'll stick together. If your oil is the right temperature — really hot — the fish will be ready as soon as the batter starts to become a darker brown around the edges. Drain on paper towels and serve immediately with lots of lemon and Bundle Hill Salad and Bundle Hill Chips (pages 202–3). Serves 4

drinking

Fish and chips and red wine? It's the ever so subtle burnt, earthy and sour taste stout gives the batter that makes it go with red wine. Flathead doesn't have a lot of oil and for that reason doesn't make red wine taste metallic. In summer time, a slightly refrigerated, mass-market merlot goes fantastically with this — don't go for anything too gung ho. If you want to be orthodox and drink white, choose a cool-climate chardonnay.

south coast noodles

This is the recipe you can pull out when the no-gluten, no-meat, no-fun people come around for dinner.

buying

2 x 500 g (1 lb 2 oz) packets of fresh rice noodles
1 tablespoon olive oil
3 garlic cloves, crushed
2 teaspoons grated ginger
$1^1/_2$ teaspoons ground cumin
1–2 small red chillies, deseeded and chopped
300 g ($10^1/_2$ oz) block of firm tofu, cut into cubes
1 head of broccoli (about 300 g/$10^1/_2$ oz), cut into little pieces
200 g (7 oz) tinned baby corn
1 bunch of baby bok choy (pak choi), chopped
3 tablespoons fish sauce
2 handfuls of snowpeas (mangetout)
425 g (15 oz) tin of tuna in oil, drained (optional, if doing the vegetarian thing)
2 tablespoons lime juice
soy sauce, to season
coriander (cilantro) leaves, to garnish

cooking

Bring a saucepan of water to the boil, add the noodles and boil for about 5 minutes until soft, or cook according to the packet instructions. Drain, rinse, then drain again and set aside.

Heat the oil in a wok over high heat. Add the garlic, ginger, cumin and chilli. Cook until fragrant — 1 or 2 minutes. Add the tofu and stir-fry it in the spices for a few minutes, then add the broccoli, baby corn and bok choy. Add the noodles and fish sauce and stir-fry for another 5 minutes. Add the snowpeas, tuna and the lime juice and cook until warmed through. Season with soy sauce and garnish with coriander. Serves 4

drinking

In keeping with its soothing nature, this stir-fry is not highly chillied. It can also be customized to suit what you want to drink. If you make it with tofu, you'll probably want to drink green tea or water. With tuna, it goes pretty well with riesling. Or if you want to drink soft reds, cook it with chicken thigh fillet or pork.

tips+tricks+tabletalk

This dish is done in a wok but it's not really a stir-fry. The vegies are not actually fried in oil — it's more of a stir-blanch. So if it looks a bit dry, it's OK to add a little bit of water.

Even if your Asian takeaway is right next door and they have their stir-fry ingredients sitting next to the wok ready to rock, you'll be able to put this on the table faster than they can. Indeed, speed is everything here. And heat. If you don't have a good wok and a good gas burner, forget it. Go next door.

buying

750 g (1 lb 10 oz) thick rump steak
2 red chillies, deseeded and very finely chopped
3 garlic cloves, pasted (see tips, page 35)
1 tablespoon olive oil
90 g (1 cup) bean sprouts
1/2 bunch of coriander (cilantro), leaves coarsely ripped up
1/2 bunch of basil, leaves only
1 tablespoon fish sauce
1 tablespoon light soy sauce, plus extra to serve

42

cooking

Slice the rump across the length into strips, and then slice those strips into strips. The longer you can make the strips of beef, the better looking the dish. Put them in a bowl, add the chillies and garlic and toss it all around.

Now, wok. Turn the gas up high. Get the wok hot! Add the oil and then immediately add the rump, in batches. Stir, toss and flip like your life depends on it. When the meat takes some brown colour and its interior is still pink, remove from the wok, then repeat with the next batch. Whatever you do, don't poach the beef in its own juices — stir-fries need to be fried in a hot and dry wok, not steamed in a wet one or the beef will go grey and chewy. When the last batch of meat is cooked, return all the meat to the wok and add everything else. Stir, toss, flip. Serve with the soy sauce and jasmine rice. Serves 4

drinking

We've done countless experiments with chilli and wine. The conclusion? Nothing actually goes with chilli, although some things are better than others. As a chilli dish, this recipe's strong point is that it is basically stir-fried steak. Steak = wine friendliness; chilli doesn't. So, how do you overcome this? Fruity, ripe, round reds survive the chilli ordeal better than angular, tannic, oaky ones. Cheap red — have a night off the serious wine.

survival

rations

survival rations

'I didn't eat spud for a week and it's a month since I tasted a bit of fish. All that's laid before me at mealtime is hunger itself and I don't even get salt with that. I ate a scrap of turf last night and I wouldn't say that this black feeding agreed too well with my belly.'

The Poor Mouth, Flann O'Brien

The modern cookbook is no longer just a compilation of recipes. There are kilojoule counts, cultural discursions, chemical analyses, biological excursions and even ridiculous wine suggestions. Goodness gracious. But while guiding our aspirational lifestyles, cookbooks invariably lack information about cooking on the cheap. Though we can't yet claim to make turf palatable (it is one of the most challenging ingredients in anyone's kitchen, although lawn clippings seem to be doing well in juice bars), we do claim to be particularly skilful at cycling and recycling inexpensive ingredients into comely comestibles.

Before we were so terribly famous (and even now that we are) we were both very familiar with the taste of poverty. Ben's done things with potato peelings and second-hand T-bones that few could imagine, let alone achieve; and Greg managed to survive for a whole month on seaweed and coastal succulents. (Talk about pigface being in your face.) Even when we did have money there were better things to spend it on — wine, women, books, guitars — than an expensive cut of meat or a trendy fish cutlet.

Between us we have half a century's experience of thrift chefing. And that's an important culinary art. Professionally trained cooks go straight into professional brigades where they are taught to cook with restaurant ingredients. They never learn the best way to cook a lamb shoulder chop — they do racks and cutlets. They don't discover how to make tough steak palatable — they grill fillet. Fish such as trout and salmon are the species with which they become familiar — they never find out how best to express the exquisite flavour of mullet or mackerel. How can they ever relate to the reader who is trying to make something from a tin of tuna and a handful of frozen peas?

The recipes in this chapter are the result of prudence, parsimony, practicality and, of course, poverty. In the interests of food science and erudition we've even conducted experiments on ourselves. The most infamous was Greg's cabbage trial. After eleven gruelling months of living on cabbage soup, cabbage rolls, cabbage au gratin, cabbage Lorraine, cabbage and rice, steamed cabbage, baked cabbage and cabbage surprise, he proved that, albeit with some weight loss, man can live on cabbage alone. There is, however, an after-effect once the diet returns to normal. It becomes very difficult to ever eat cabbage again — in any form. For that reason you won't see a cabbage recipe in this chapter (thrifty vegetable though it is), but you will find plenty of other fine survival fare. Remember — in poverty, there can still lie grace.

carbonara

Why is it that the simple things in life so quickly become corrupted? Twelve-bar blues, yoghurt, hair styles…and recipes. This is one of the easiest recipes in the world, but it is also one of the most abused. Chefs and cooks in all sorts of pubs, cafés and fine dining establishments don't seem to know when to stop. As a result, you get carbonara with chilli, carbonara with truffle oil, carbonara with salami and, perhaps most offensive and morally corrupt of all, carbonara made with cream. Ask yourself this simple question: would you put cream on your eggs and bacon? This pasta is very quick to prepare, invariably all the ingredients are close at hand, and it's a great hangover lunch.

48

400 g (14 oz) pasta, such as spaghetti, linguine or fettucine
5 rashers of bacon, rind removed, finely sliced
1 tablespoon olive oil
1 garlic clove, pasted (see tips, page 35)
4 eggs
1 tablespoon unsalted butter
15 g (1/2 cup) roughly chopped flat-leaf (Italian) parsley, to garnish
100 g (1 cup) grated Parmigiano Reggiano cheese

cooking

Bring a large saucepan of water to a rolling boil. Add 1 teaspoon salt and throw in the pasta. Cook the pasta according to the packet instructions.

Put a large non-stick frying pan on high heat. Add the bacon and olive oil. Once browned, add the pasted garlic and stir everything around until the garlic has just taken on a golden colour — don't burn it in any way whatsoever! Remove the pan from the heat.

Drain the pasta in a colander, reserving some of the cooking water, and return the pasta to the saucepan along with the bacon and garlic. Break the eggs into the pasta (over no heat) and mix everything around. Add the butter. Another stir. Timing is critical with carbonara: don't let it become too dried out when you are in the final assembly stage. If it looks too dry, add a few tablespoons of reserved pasta water when mixing it together. How much you stir everything through will affect the consistency: for a wet carbonara, don't overwork the eggs; for a drier finish, stir it through for longer. It's up to you really.

Serve onto heated plates or bowls. Parsley garnish. And as much grated Parmigiano as you can take, or your holistic medical practitioner allows. Serves 4

49

drinking

Some of the simplest foods are the hardest to find the right wine for. This dish is no more than eggs and bacon with spag chucked through it. And what do you drink with E & B? Coffee? Tea? No. Austere white wine is the go here. Flinty wine. Italian pinot grigio without too much fruit power or Australian semillon/chardonnay blends that are not too rich. Remember, this dish is unsophisticated, so keep your wine the same. For reds, use dolcetto that isn't too sweet, Montepulciano d'Abruzzo or some unwooded, cheap cabernet sauvignon. Nothing too fresh and fruity.

carbonara

chicken fricassee

There's something very satisfying about chopping up a whole chicken and turning the resultant pieces into a fricassee. And it's relatively quick to make, too. The key ingredient in this dish is the white wine vinegar, which adds a piquancy that lifts and heightens the chicken's flavour. The other great thing about this recipe is that you can do it all in one pot. So when you can't be bothered waiting for the oven to reach its ideal operating temperature or when it is raining on the barbecue, fricassee, fricassee, fricassee.

chicken fricassee

buying

1 chicken
2 tablespoons olive oil
1 tablespoon unsalted butter
1 tablespoon plain (all-purpose) flour
2 rashers of bacon, rind removed, finely chopped
1 onion, roughly chopped
1 carrot, roughly chopped
1 celery stalk, roughly chopped
2 garlic cloves, finely chopped
2 tablespoons white wine vinegar
375 ml (1 1/2 cups) chicken stock
a few sprigs of sage or thyme

cooking

If you are unfamiliar with the anatomy of a chook, now is the time to become more intimate. Chop the chicken into eight pieces (or ask the butcher to joint the bird for you). To do this yourself, use kitchen scissors, poultry shears or a sharp knife to trim off the wing tips. Discard them. Put the chicken breast-side up on a chopping board. To remove the legs, cut through the loose skin between the leg and breastbone. Cut down to the joint, then twist the leg away from the body. Cut through the ball and socket joint. Cut each leg in half through the joint, to separate the thigh from the drumstick. Next, holding the breast, cut along the natural break in the rib cage (down where you cut the legs from the breast) and lift the breast from the lower carcass (keep the carcass for stock or discard). Put the breast on the chopping board and press firmly along the breastbone to break it. To cut the breast in half, cut along the breastbone and through the wishbone. Cut the wings from the breast, leaving a little breast meat on each one. You should have eight pieces.

Put a large frying pan or casserole dish onto the stove. Medium heat. Add the olive oil and butter. Dust the jointed chicken with the flour. Turn the heat to high and brown the chicken pieces four at a time. Reduce the heat to medium once the pan is starting to produce some el scorchio effects. Remove the final pieces of chicken from the pan and add the bacon. Cook for 3 minutes, then add the vegetables and garlic. Stir all of this about and cook for another 5 minutes.

Return all the chicken pieces to the pan. Turn the heat up high, splash in the wine vinegar and stir everything about again. Add the stock and the herbs, bring the fricassee back to a simmer, reduce the heat to very, very, very low and — leaving the lid ajar — cook on top of the stove for 45 minutes to 1 hour, or until the chicken is cooked through. (If the pan gets too dry at any stage, add a few tablespoons of water.) Good with rice. Serves 4

53

drinking

Piquant is the key word here. That dismisses most of Australia's red and white fare. Italian grape varieties are the kings and queens (or *re* and *regina*) of piquancy. It's all to do with the tannins and acids and the way they form the structure or skeleton of the wine. This allows the wine to envelop the fricasseed chook; not the other way around. Sangiovese is a good grape variety to choose.

tips+tricks+tabletalk

Don't be afraid to cook this dish fairly dry — too much liquid can bleach out the chicken's flavours.

As with most things in life, more is not better: don't overdo the white wine vinegar. If you can just taste the difference, then you've added just the right amount.

This soup is best eaten the day after it's made, and will last for three days in the fridge, no worries. From whence it came, it will happily return. Why should the compost heap get all the good stuff?

minestre alla fridge

buying

The trick is not to buy anything. You've already bought it — weeks ago.
But in an ideal world the ingredients list would look something like this:

2 tablespoons olive oil
1 large carrot, roughly diced
2 celery stalks, ditto
1 leek, finely sliced
1 onion, finely diced
100 g ($3^1/_2$ oz) green beans, topped and tailed
2 peeled desiree potatoes, 1 finely diced, 1 very roughly diced
200 g (7 oz) mixed dried beans
2 garlic cloves, pasted (see tips, page 35)
400 g (14 oz) tin of tomatoes
1.5 litres (6 cups) beef stock
freshly grated Parmigiano Reggiano cheese, to serve

cooking

You will need a large heavy-based saucepan or cast-iron casserole dish — you don't want the ingredients to catch and burn on the bottom of the pan. Medium heat, the olive oil, then add all the ingredients as listed, except the cheese, stirring between each addition.

Bring the mixture to the boil, then simmer with the lid on for 1 hour. If at any stage the soup becomes too dry, simply top up with water. Grated Parmigiano is good on top when served. Bread and plenty of wine. Serves 4

drinking

Beef stock, tomatoes and long cooking make this a soup for red wine. Anything savoury in flavour will suit. Beware of too much oak in any wine. Semi-decaying reds, like the vegetables you have used, are good, as are cheaper, lighter blends of cabernet and shiraz-dominant wines.

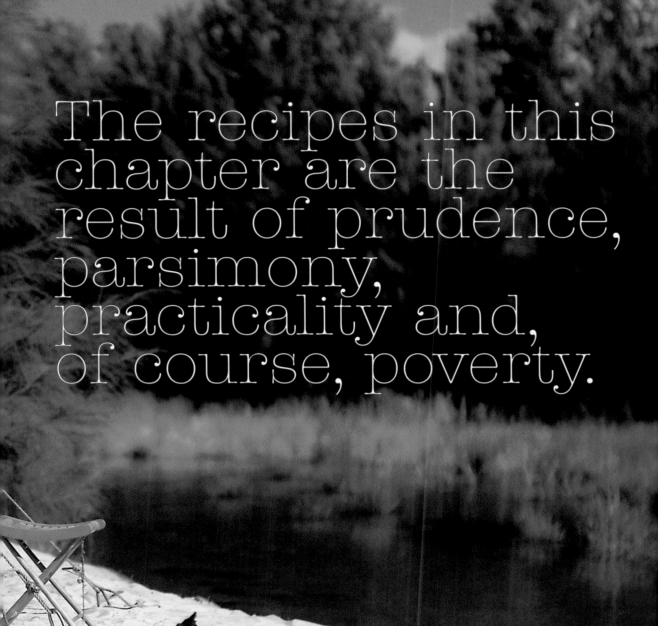

The recipes in this chapter are the result of prudence, parsimony, practicality and, of course, poverty.

If you're feeling wan, crook or just plain hungover, there is nothing better than this soup. It's basically a clear beef broth with the zingy freshness of ginger and the comfort of noodles.

revivifying ginger and beef noodle soup

buying

1 kg (2 lb 4 oz) shin (gravy) beef
1 large thumb of ginger, peeled and sliced into thin rounds
1 large onion, diced
250 g (9 oz) dried Chinese egg or wheat noodles
2 spring onions (scallions), sliced on the diagonal

cooking

Cut the beef into 1¹⁄₂ cm (⁵⁄₈ inch) cubes, removing as much fat as possible. Fill a large saucepan two-thirds full with cold water. High heat, then add the beef. Three large pinches of salt and three good grinds of black pepper. Then add the ginger and onion. When the water comes to the boil, reduce to a simmer and skim the frothy, yukky stuff off the surface of the liquid. This will take a while, but it's worth it to have a clear soup. Put the lid on, slightly ajar, and simmer as low as possible for 1–1¹⁄₂ hours, or until the beef is very tender.

Cook the noodles separately until just cooked. Drain and add the noodles to large bowls, then ladle the soup over the top. Garnish with the spring onions. Serves 4

58

drinking

This is a soup that is surprisingly wine friendly, especially after it has cooled down a little in the bowl. The main flavour is that zesty zing of the ginger. The best thing for it is light, fruity reds: cheap merlot or good Italian dolcetto. Failing that, go for an everyday red wine that is not too serious and not too tannic.

The trouble with some famous dishes, such as cassoulet, is the way some people get so cranky about the recipe's interpretation. (Bouillabaisse, the fish stew from Marseilles, is probably the most famous example.) Besides, if recipes cannot emigrate, immigrate, evolve and adapt, who or what can? We just have to accept that the world is full of authentic replicas. Here's our version of cassoulet, the bean and sausage stew of France's Languedoc region.

benandgregoulet

375 g (13 oz) packet of dried haricot beans,
    or 2 x 400 g (14 oz) tins of haricot beans
2 pork spare ribs, cut into eight pieces
4 chicken drumsticks
4 good quality sausages
plain (all-purpose) flour, for dusting
3 tablespoons olive oil
3 garlic cloves, pasted (see tips, page 35)
1 onion, roughly diced
1 carrot, ditto
1 celery stalk, ditto
1 tablespoon tomato paste (purée)
2 tablespoons white wine vinegar
750 ml (3 cups) chicken stock

cooking

Start this survival staple by preparing the beans. If using dried beans, bring them to the boil in a large saucepan of water and simmer for 15 minutes, then turn off the heat and let them soak for 1 hour. Once this is done, you can get stuck in. Or you can cheat and fast track this dish by using tinned beans. Drain them and set aside.

Preheat the oven to 150°C (300°F/Gas 2). Dust the ribs, drumsticks and sausages lightly in the flour. Then you'll need to get a large flameproof casserole dish on the stove. Medium heat. Add the olive oil and brown the spare ribs pieces for about 10 minutes. They need to be a little crispy. Remove them, then lightly brown the drumsticks and then the sausages. If the base of the dish is getting too burnt, reduce the heat to low. Set all the meat aside.

Now add the garlic, vegetables and tomato paste. Stir this all about, turn up the heat to high, add half the meat, the wine vinegar and the stock. Throw in the drained beans and the rest of the meat. If the liquid level does not just cover the solids, top up with water. Stir everything about, pop on the lid and then into the oven for about 2 hours. (If you are using tinned beans, you'll only need to cook this for 1 hour.) The cooking time is bean dependent. The little buggers have a will of their own — be careful not to overcook them and turn them into mash, but make sure they aren't still bits of lead shot after the oven cooking. A green salad is optional. Otherwise, lotsa wine and some crusty bread. Serves 4

drinking

Blended, gruff, tannic red monsters can be subdued effortlessly with this all-conquering bean stew — grenache and shiraz amalgams or Rhône blends. Fats alone need tannins to dissect them and render them digestible, but the farinaceous quality of this dish means you can opt for more generous, warm, round and alcoholic wines, such as big company Barossa shiraz.

This recipe is found all over Italy. It is the ultimate survival meal. It tastes like food from a posh Italian restaurant but costs virtually nothing to make.

buying

8 sage leaves

100 g (3^1/$_2$ oz) pancetta, in one piece (if you're broke or you can't get pancetta, bacon will suffice)

3 garlic cloves, roughly chopped, plus 1 whole garlic clove

3 tablespoons good olive oil

2 celery stalks, sliced

5 Roma (plum) tomatoes, chopped

2 litres (8 cups) homemade chicken stock, or the stuff in cartons

375 g (13 oz) dried cannellini beans (sometimes labelled as Great Northern beans), soaked overnight, then drained

4 slices of crusty Italian bread, wood-fired is good, thickly sliced

freshly ground black pepper

cooking

In a large heavy-based saucepan put the sage, pancetta, the 3 chopped garlic cloves and 2 tablespoons of the olive oil. Cook over a low heat until the garlic is golden. Be careful not to smash up the sage leaves when you're stirring. Add the celery, tomatoes, chicken stock and the beans and bring to a simmer. Simmer with the lid on until the beans are tender. That should take 1^1/$_2$ – 2^1/$_2$ hours, depending on the age of your beans.

Take out the chunk of pancetta and put it aside. Remove half the solids from the saucepan and purée them. Return the purée to the pan. Roughly slice the pancetta and put that in too.

In a 180°C (350°F/Gas 4) oven, toast the bread until golden. Cut the remaining garlic clove in half and rub one side of the toast with the garlic. Put the toast garlic-side up in the bottom of deep bowls and drizzle with the remaining olive oil. Pour the soup on top. Pepper. Serve. Serves 4, with ample leftovers

65

drinking

Soup and wine rarely works well as a combo. It's the whole liquid-and-liquid scenario. But this soup is almost like beans on toast — and it has some very wine-friendly flavours: olive oil, chicken stock, sage, pancetta, the puréed beans and plenty of garlic. It's fantastic with lightish reds. The best ones are Italian. Cheap Chianti. Rustic Australian shiraz and shiraz cabernet blends are good too.

aussie berko

Aussie or osso?

One of our core brand values is that recipes aren't static. You can help them to evolve — like God does with us. Here we've changed an Italian classic by swapping a few ingredients — principally, beef instead of veal.

buying

1 tablespoon plain (all-purpose) flour
4 pieces of gravy beef 'ossobuco' — beef, not veal
1–2 tablespoons olive oil
1 carrot, roughly chopped
1 celery stalk, roughly chopped
2 garlic cloves, finely chopped
a small handful of whatever fresh herbs you can find
half a tin of Italian tomatoes (200 g/7 oz), roughly chopped
375 ml (1 1/2 cups) bottle of good quality Aussie stout (Coopers or Southwark)

cooking

Preheat the oven to 150°C (300°F/Gas 2). Put the flour in the plastic bag holding the meat. Mix it all around. Heat a flameproof casserole dish over medium heat and add a thin coating of olive oil. Brown the meat, take it out, then put in the chopped vegies, the garlic and herbs. Cook for about 6 minutes. Return the meat to the dish and turn the heat up to flat-out.

Add the tomatoes and beer, stir it all together and bring back to a gentle simmer. Put the lid on. Bang it in the oven for 90 minutes (turn the meat over once during cooking), or until the meat is just starting to come away from the central bone. And be sure to eat the marrow in the middle — it's good for you. Serves 4

drinking

Stout could be the drink for this in really cold weather but, if you are a wine addict, this is the dish for all those dead reds you've got in your cellar. Try some Hunter Valley shiraz with a bit of age on it. Or if you've got only enough money to buy a brand new sub-ten dollar red, buy South Australian shiraz.

tips+tricks+tabletalk

Gravy beef ossobuco? Stout? Australian butchers and supermarkets call slices of beef shin (where gravy beef comes from) 'ossobuco'. It's not ossobuco. The real thing comes from the same part of the animal but from veal, not beef. And the stout? This adds a rich yet savoury and bitter twist to the dish.

chinese sporks with arrogance

Spare ribs — or sporks, as we lovingly call them — are a cheap pork cut but have a certain luxuriousness and plenty of flavour. Best of all they're not lean, and when cooked this way they don't taste like shoe leather. Serve with couscous and a simple salad.

buying

- 1 teaspoon ground cumin
- 1 teaspoon ground fenugreek
- 1 teaspoon ground coriander
- 4 star anise
- 1 tablespoon olive oil
- 4–8 pork spare ribs, depending on their size and your hunger
- 2 tablespoons sherry vinegar
- 2 tablespoons soy sauce

cooking

Throw the spices into a heavy-based saucepan and turn the heat to high. When the spices begin to release their aroma, pour on the olive oil and very quickly add the sporks. Reduce the heat to medium and cook until the sporks are caramel in colour and crusty on the bottom side. Turn them over and add half the vinegar and half the soy. Reduce the heat to low and put the lid on.

Cook for 15 minutes, then add the remaining vinegar, soy sauce and 125 ml (1/2 cup) hot water. Cook for a further 10 minutes. If, at any stage during this cooking process, the base of the pan begins to burn, add a little more water. Remove the star anise before serving. Serves 4

drinking

Unlike a lot of cuts of pork, sporks offer no ambiguity in the colour of wine they demand. Red. It's the fat. It needs the structure and grip of a red wine to keep your tastebuds upright. So what reds? Cheap pinot, dry South Australian cabernet merlot or, arguably, Australia's most underrated wine style, South Australian shiraz cabernet.

In a perfect world this is what a meat pie would be like, wherever you bought one: at a milk bar, a service station or at the footy. Ideally, this same football ground would serve well-priced bottle-aged Hunter Valley shiraz. A two-bottle limit. This recipe is basically two recipes combined: the pie's filling (a slow-cooked beef casserole) and the pastry (an edible container). The tricky bit is to have your pie filling cooked and ready a day, or half a day, before you put it in the pastry case.

shin beef pie

buying

for the beef casserole:
1 kg (2 lb 4 oz) shin (gravy) beef, cut into medium cubes
60 g (1/2 cup) plain (all-purpose) flour
1 tablespoon olive oil
3 small red onions, peeled and quartered
3 rashers of bacon, rind removed, roughly chopped
15 button mushrooms, halved
250 ml (1 cup) red wine
beef stock or water

for the pastry:
250 g (2 cups) plain (all-purpose) flour
150 g (51/2 oz) cold unsalted butter, cubed
2 eggs, lightly beaten
lemon juice
about 1 tablespoon milk

cooking

Start by making the casserole. Preheat the oven to 120°C (230°F/Gas 1). Toss the cubed beef in the flour, then brown the pieces in a frying pan with the olive oil over medium to high heat. Once browned, transfer to a casserole dish. Add the onions and bacon to the frying pan and cook until browned. Chuck into the casserole, along with the mushrooms.

Pour the red wine into the frying pan and scrape up all the good bits from the base of the pan, then let it simmer for about 10 minutes, or until the liquid is reduced by half. Add to the casserole as well. Using stock or water, make sure the casserole dish is about one-third filled with liquid. Cover. Put into the oven for 2–3 hours. Slow cooking. Allow to cool completely once cooked.

Now for the pastry. Into a food processor (with the blade in), tip the flour, cubed butter and a sprinkle of salt. Use the 'pulse' button to turn these ingredients into a coarse sort of breadcrumby, dry mixture. About 5 or 6 whizz-whizzes should do it. Pour in the beaten eggs, a squeeze of lemon juice and 1 tablespoon of water — now run the processor until the mixture becomes dough. Tip it out into a plastic bag, shape into a disc and put in the freezer for 10 minutes.

Preheat the oven to 170°C (325°F/Gas 3). Divide the pastry into two pieces: one-third and two-thirds. Roll out a lid using the smaller piece and then roll out the liner for your favourite pie tin (of about 2 litres/ 8 cup capacity) with the other piece. Line the pie tin with the pastry.

Pour a touch of milk into the base of the lined pie tin and swirl around. Add the cold stew mixture (if it seems quite liquidy, don't add all the liquid or the pie will be soggy). Cover with the pastry lid, press the sides together artistically and brush with milk. Make a small slit in the centre to allow steam to escape. Bake in the oven for 45 minutes. Let it stand for 10 minutes before you cut it. Mashed spuds and peas, tomato sauce or mustard, and loads of red wine. Serves 4

70

drinking

The thing that makes this meat pie so good with red wine is the gelatinous nature of the shin beef. This lines the mouth and gives you an impression of sustenance — but you do need red wine to strip it off. This is why it suits savoury, spicy shiraz. To adapt this dish to pinot noir, add more mushrooms and bacon at the expense of the beef.

This whole catastrophe can be made the day before you want it, or on the weekend. Be sure to make the mixture for the pie filling reasonably wet if you are going to keep it in the fridge for a few days, otherwise it will be too dry after reheating (fridges are very dry places). Reheat the pie in a cold-start oven, allowing the pie to come up to speed with the rising temperature of the oven.

tonno in scatola insalata

The thing that defines a good recipe is how long it stays in your repertoire. Ever since Greg stole this salad from an old girlfriend back in the early 1990s, it has never left the menu at La Maison de Duncan Powell. It's light and really good with wine.

buying

2 eggs
2 medium waxy potatoes (pink-eyes are good), unpeeled
1 garlic clove, squashed
1 large red onion, sliced into thin rings
2 small zucchinis (courgettes), sliced
about 1 tablespoon olive oil
1 cos (romaine) lettuce, torn into pieces
2 celery stalks, chopped
95 g (1/2 cup) Kalamata or Ligurian olives
425 g (15 oz) tin of tuna in oil
good quality balsamic vinegar, to serve
good quality extra virgin olive oil, to serve (optional)

cooking

Put the eggs in a small saucepan of gently simmering water. Cook for 7 minutes. Roughly crack their shells and cool under cold running water. Cook the potatoes in boiling water for about 15 minutes until tender. Cool under cold running water.

Meanwhile, take a large salad bowl or plate and rub the inside with the squashed garlic. In a non-stick frying pan, fry the onion and zucchini in just enough oil so that they burn a little bit. Set aside to cool. Peel and slice the eggs. Dice the potatoes. Put the cos into the salad bowl. Add the eggs, potatoes, celery and olives. Flake the tuna and add it to the bowl, oil and all. Garnish with the onion rings and zucchini slices. Splash with really good balsamic and olive oil (if using) once it's plated. Serves 4

drinking

There's a fair bit going on in this salad — potato, fishiness, egginess — so aromatic whites such as riesling and sauvignon blanc tend to be overpowered. Firm, young white wines with no wood, not too much flavour and plenty of acid, such as pinot grigio or young marsanne, are the ones that work. Best of all is a dry, fresh, zingy rosé.

There is nothing exotic about the forequarter chop, or barbecue chop as butchers call them. But the addition of a few spices, some yoghurt and some slow cooking can transform them into succulent, fragrant morsels.

buying

8 forequarter lamb chops, trimmed of excess fat
2 teaspoons olive oil
1 large onion, finely diced
3 garlic cloves, finely chopped
1 tablespoon very finely chopped ginger
2 large green chillies, deseeded and finely chopped
2 tomatoes, roughly chopped
1¹/₂ teaspoons ground cumin
1¹/₂ teaspoons ground coriander
¹/₂ teaspoon ground turmeric
8 cardamom pods, crushed open with the side of a knife
200 g (7 oz) tub of natural yoghurt

cooking

Preheat the oven to 150°C (300°F/Gas 2). Chop each chop in half. (A Chinese cleaver is useful.) Medium heat. Put the oil in a heavy-based casserole dish and brown the chops in batches. Add extra oil, if needed. Once the lamb is browned, remove to a side plate. Add the onion, garlic, ginger and chilli and cook until the onion is transparent.

Reduce the heat to low, add the tomatoes and spices and cook uncovered, stirring occasionally, until the tomato breaks down and becomes pulpy — about 5 minutes. Remove the casserole from the heat and mix the yoghurt through. (Add the yoghurt off the heat or it may boil and separate. Yuk.) Spoon out the contents into a food whizzer or blender and whizz until you've got a semi-smooth mixture. Don't clean the whizzer just yet.

Arrange the chop halves in the bottom of the casserole and spoon the blended tomato and yoghurt mixture over them. Rinse out the whizzer with 125 ml (¹/₂ cup) water, swill this around and pour it into the casserole. Cover. Oven for 75 minutes. Adjust the thickness of the curry at the end by adding a few tablespoons of water, if needed. Serve with rice (see Crunchy Granola Rice, page 209) and a green salad. Serves 4

drinking

Strangely enough, this is a red meat curry that actually goes well with white wine. A rich semillon/sauvignon blanc blend is a surprisingly good partner: it cuts through the fat left clinging to your lips. If you want to drink red, try a cheapo cabernet.

tonno in scatola insalata

saggy lamb curry

deep sea bacon

Here's another way to turn fish into red wine food. Not only can these skewers be prepared ahead of time, they're also effortless to cook. It's also one of the best ways to lightly infuse into your main ingredient the otherwise toxic power of fresh rosemary.

buying

4 fish fillets: blue eye cod, flathead or John dory
4 long sprigs of rosemary
2 rashers of streaky bacon, cut in half
4 wooden skewers
4 teaspoons Dijon mustard
olive oil
1/2 lemon
sea salt and freshly ground black pepper

77

cooking

Fold each fish fillet in half and secure it by threading a rosemary sprig through the doubled-up end and out the other. Lay a bacon rasher half on top of each fillet and fix this in place with a skewer.

Preheat the griller (broiler) to high. Smear a level teaspoon of mustard over each skewered fish fillet and put it bacon-side down on a baking tray that's been loosely lined with foil. Drizzle some oil over the fish, squeeze a half lemon over everything and season with salt and pepper.

Pop under the hot griller, going flat stick. Grill (broil) for 3 minutes and turn over, exposing the bacon to the griller's savage heat. Continue grilling until the bacon is cooked and the fish is just tender, about 4–5 minutes, depending on the size of the fillets. Plate. Carefully pour any juice over the fish. Serves 4

drinking

Bacon and mustard, not to mention rosemary's pungency, make this a good dish for pinot noir. Subtle, dry cabernet merlot blends (preferably from cooler regions) can also work well. Spanish reds, like tempranillo, are also crackers with this fish.

A fresh bay leaf is another idea here. Place it in the fold of the fillet.

Rosemary should be mostly avoided in hand-to-hand food combat. Never add it to salads or to fricassees, and in stews a few leaves are all that's needed. Rosemary really is a weapon of mass destruction when used like a herb.

illegal

lunches

illegal lunches

'Some weasel took a cork out of my lunch.'

You Can't Cheat An Honest Man, W.C. Fields

Lunch — in its myriad guises — can offer you so much. There's the tête-à-tête lunch, the recovery lunch, the business lunch, the first date lunch, the quiet solo lunch, the picnic, the barbecue... And eating a substantial meal in the middle of the day is good for you. Indeed, most of our western twenty-first century diseases, such as cancer, obesity, heart disease and RSI, can be traced to an imbalance between lunch and dinner. When we worshipped the sun and not the fluoro or halogen Gods, we ate more healthily. People died from the Black Plague, equestrian accidents or sword thrusts, not from myocardial infarcts or colon cancers.

A common complaint is that eating a substantial lunch makes you tired. This is exactly what's meant to happen. Your body is talking to you. Listen. Most of the grumpiness and general nastiness people inflict on each other every day is a result of no afternoon sleep — you know how kids get if they don't have a lie down. If everyone in Australia had a rest from 2 to 3 p.m. as a point of protest, it would only take a few weeks and the Federal government would be forced to legislate in favour of a national siesta and Australia would be a much less cantankerous place. We'd need our own word, of course. 'Arvo' could be good. 'No, madam, these shoes will not be ready until this evening; you can pick them up after arvo.'

But because this is not a reality and is unlikely ever to be one, lunches have an air of illegality or illicitness about them. If you talk of having lunch, and having lunch midweek with a few glasses of wine, well, people start looking at you askance. Women draw their jackets closer to them; men adjust their spectacles and cough a single, nervous cough. Dogs sense what's going on and, heads low and tails at half-mast, silently scamper out of the room to the safety of a nearby four-lane highway. Lunch — when it's not one of those gruelling, for-my-sins-Lord-I-must-suffer family ones — is meant to be short, sharp, safe and sober. And a salad sandwich.

Clearly, this situation will not do. If only for your health, at every opportunity you should eat a two or three course lunch and drink at least half a bottle of wine. Of course, if your work-slavery doesn't allow this kind of health regime, then you've got to get lunch into your life on every weekend and rostered day off. And if you've got any concerns about what a T-bone and half a bottle of cabernet will do to you at 1 p.m., get over it. That's what the afternoon is for — plodding around the house/office/garden in a slightly giddy, well-fed state.

If nothing else, we earnestly hope that this book — and, more specifically, this chapter — will inspire a reappraisal of the luncheon and, possibly, even a rediscovery. Lunch can help us solve most of the problems of the world, and a few personal ones, too.

scotch fillet

When in need of protein and the essential amino acids required to run our bodies, when our hair or nails won't grow, or when we have to drink young cabernet, scotch fillet is the answer. It is the most forgiving of all steak cuts in terms of its flavour, tenderness and its unique unstuffupableness.

buying

4 scotch fillet steaks (about 200–225 g/7–8 oz each), as thick
    as you can get them or as thick as you dare. We think 4 cm
    (1 1/2 inches) is a minimum thickness, at lunch. Dinner is a
    different matter...
sea salt and freshly ground black pepper
Dijon mustard

cooking

Whatever cooking aparatus you are using, get it hot. Red hot. So warm up the barbecue or heat the chargrill pan. Once it is at operational temperature, add the steaks and LEAVE THEM ALONE. Do not give in to the temptation to move them or turn them or flatten them out with the barbie tools.

Cook the steak until beads of liquid begin to appear on the top. Turn the meat and cook for half the time it's taken you to cook the first side. Turn off the heat and let the steak sit for 2 minutes. If cooking on a barbecue or if your pan is still very hot after the cooking is finished, move the steaks to a cooler spot. Letting the meat rest after the cooking process is critical, so put it on a warm plate and leave it for another couple of minutes. It gets a chance to relax and is then less likely to bleed on your plate. It'll also be more tender. Plate. Salt, pepper, mustard. Serve with chips (see Bundle Hill Chips, page 203). Serves 4

drinking

Cabernet sauvignon or cabernet blends. The best you can get your hands on — Bordeaux, or Western Australian, Clare Valley or Central Victoria. If you've got young cabernet that is smelling and tasting of a bit too much oak, just use more mustard. Scotch fillet's pockets of fat and cabernet's tannins are a marriage made in heaven.

tuna and broad bean penne

You should never eat luncheon on the run. It is your right as a human being to be able to sit down to a bowl of pasta and a couple of glasses of vino, no matter what chaos is going on around you.

buying

500 g (1 lb 2 oz) dried penne
200 g (7¹/₂ oz) frozen broad (fava) beans
1 tablespoon olive oil
2 red onions, cut into thin rings
425 g (15 oz) tin of tuna in oil
80 g (¹/₂ cup) pitted black olives, preferably Kalamata
4 anchovies, roughly chopped
2 tablespoons lemon juice
freshly ground black pepper
2 tablespoons roughly chopped flat-leaf (Italian) parsley

cooking

Get a big saucepan of well-salted water on the heat. When it's boiling, add the penne and broad beans. In a non-stick frying pan, add the olive oil and fry up the onion rings. When the penne is al dente and the beans are cooked, quickly drain the pasta and the beans, reserving the hot water to warm the pasta bowls — this dish needs to be hot.

Increase the heat under the frying pan so that the onions are sizzling. Then turn it off and add the tuna with the oil from the tin. Throw in the olives, the broad beans and pasta, the anchovies and lemon juice. Mix it all about, then season with pepper. You won't need salt because the anchovies already give it a bit of saltiness. Garnish with parsley. Eat. Serves 4

drinking

There's an Italian red wine made from the grape variety Montepulciano d'Abruzzo that goes fantastically with this pasta at lunch. It's cheap, savoury, not too alcoholic and really easy to drink. If you can't get that, a cheap Aussie shiraz or even decent cask stuff will suffice.

Penne seems to work best here because it picks up the chunks of tuna well, hiding some of them inside their tubes. But any shape of pasta you've got in the cupboard will do — except dried lasagne sheets.

spreadeagled lamb

It's ridiculous that men and women actually pay people to take them off into the bush to discover their 'primitive side'. Simply butterflying a leg of lamb at home will achieve exactly the same thing. For free. And it garners no small amount of respect from your guests. Besides, why should we accept the leg of lamb the way God made it? By removing the bone and laying the meat out flat you get to cook the leg meat both from the inside and out. It's a great lamb dish for those who like the crusty, well-done bits — you know, those bits of which there never seem to be enough on a conventional roasted leg.

buying

1 leg of lamb, boned and butterflied
4 garlic cloves, pasted (see tips, page 35)
2 tablespoons olive oil
1 tablespoon lemon juice
rock salt and freshly ground black pepper

cooking

If you're not prepared to bone the leg of lamb yourself, ask your butcher to do it, and if he won't, go to a butcher who will. By boned and butterflied we mean that the bone is removed from the leg, leaving you with a roughly square and more or less uniformly thick layer of meat.

Now, for those of us willing to attempt butterflying the lamb. Using a sharp knife, cut around the exposed ball and socket joint between the hip bone and main leg bone. Free it from the meat. Cut completely around the pelvic bone and remove it. Beginning at the top of the exposed leg bone, cut down along the bone through the meat. Using short, quick strokes, scrape the meat from the bone all around. Continue cutting along the length of the shank bone, cutting and scraping the meat away — the bone should be almost free. Lift out the leg bone and cut around the knee joint, freeing the bone completely. Remove as many tendons as possible.

Put all the other ingredients in the griller (broiler) tray, add the lamb and flip it around a few times to get it well covered with the flavouring agents. With the butterflied leg fat-side down, put the tray under the griller and, whether gas or electric, turn it to high. Don't put the top surface of the lamb too close to the flame or electric element. We like the el scorchio effect, but no one likes to eat incinerated introduced fauna. Grill (broil) for 10 minutes, turn the lamb over and cook for another 15 minutes. If the lamb begins to burn, the tray begins to dry out or burn, or flames appear to be coming from the stove, don't panic. Simply add 80 ml (1/3 cup) of water to the tray.

Turn off the griller. Leave the lamb to rest for 5 minutes. Transfer to a big board, rest for another 5 minutes before carving and eating with Potato Dauphinois (page 208) or Spudski (page 207). Serves 4

drinking

Because this is more like a huge lamb chop or kebab than a roast leg, it demands more rustic and tannic red wine. This is a good time to serve your surly or more brutish cabernets. Those wines that don't have any pretensions to elegance or finesse. Failing that, turn to the more affordable delights of cheap Australian blends. Those ones that don't cost any more than a leg of lamb.

tips+tricks+tabletalk

Instead of lemon juice, use sherry vinegar or red wine vinegar. A bit of balsamic could also give this an Italian twist.

To turn it North African or subcontinental Indian, add some ground spices to the marinade in the griller (broiler) tray. If you've got dodgy red wine, this will help all concerned — you, the lamb, the grog.

blue eye for red wine

Most complex and advanced cultures, such as the Greek, Portuguese and Tasmanian, know that it's OK to drink red with fish.

buying

4 blue eye cod cutlets
1 tablespoon plain (all-purpose) flour
1 scant teaspoon unsalted butter or olive oil
4 saffron threads
1 sprig of rosemary
sea salt and freshly ground black pepper
80 ml (1/3 cup) French dry vermouth, such as Noilly Prat

cooking

Get a large non-stick frying pan as hot as you can. (Yes, this is another recipe that only works if the smoke alarm goes off.) Very lightly sprinkle the cutlets on both sides with the flour. Add the butter or olive oil to the pan and then immediately drop in the cutlets. There'll be a bit of smoke and blackened butter or oil, but don't worry. Reduce the heat to medium and cook the cutlets for 4 minutes.

Place a saffron thread on each cutlet, a few leaves of rosemary, sprinkle with some salt and pepper and turn over. Cook for 4 more minutes. Splash on the vermouth, being careful not to get singed by any resultant alcohol flame. Cook until the liquid has reduced by half. Artistically place the fish cutlets on warm plates. Serve with steamed or boiled spuds that have been tossed with some mustard. Serves 4

drinking

There are several things in this blue eye that make it red-wine compatible. 1) Saffron: its earthy, manly, exotic fragrance helps to marry the fish flavour with red wine. 2) Rosemary: a flavour associated with red meat. 3) El scorchio: burnt fats in the hot pan. 4) Vermouth: herbal muskiness. 5) Mustard spuds... Grenache of the more sombre, savoury and costly type is great with this, and Spanish tempranillos rock, as does Ocker shiraz — stick to $20 examples.

When we worshipped the sun and not the fluoro or halogen Gods, we ate more healthily.

sunday tortilla

Eggs and Sunday just seem to go together.
And if you've not had your standard two
poached eggs for breakfast, then this is a
good lunch.

buying

2 waxy potatoes, such as desiree, Nicola, Dutch cream
2 red onions, cut into thin rings
2 tablespoons olive oil
1 chorizo sausage, sliced as thick or thin as suits
   your mood
8 eggs
a handful of roughly chopped flat-leaf (Italian) parsley
sea salt and freshly ground black pepper

cooking

Boil the spuds in their jackets until they're just cooked through. Drain
and cool them on the side of the sink.

In a non-stick frying pan over high heat, brown the onion rings in half
the olive oil. After 1 minute, add the chorizo. Meanwhile, slice the spuds
into discs and beat the eggs laconically with a fork. By now the onion
and chorizo will be done — a little bit of scorch is OK. Remove them
from the pan, wipe the base and add the remaining oil. Adjust the heat
to medium and pour in the eggs. When they have started to set, arrange
the chorizo and onion in the mixture, add the potato, parsley, sea salt,
a few twists of the pepper mill, and encourage everything to cuddle up
with a spatula, pushing the ingredients down into the egg mixture.

Put the griller (broiler) on high. Flash the tortilla under it until the top
is browned and set. Slice. Serve hot or at room temp. Salad. Serves 4

drinking

Eggs are supposed to ruin the flavour of wine. Rubbish. They
are a fantastic vehicle for flavours that go with wine. Our
tortilla is custom-made for a Spanish red such as a cheap
tempranillo from Ribera del Duero, or a Montepulciano
d'Abruzzo from Italy. Substitute bacon and mushrooms for
the chorizo and onion, and it'll prefer light pinot.

Waxy potatoes are best for this recipe as they maintain their structural integrity during the cooking process, and they're chewier in the finished dish.

tips+tricks+tabletalk

pipi spaghetti

Pipis, or vongole, are little clams. This is an easy, pretty cheap and impressive pasta dish, well suited to hotter weather or what we nowadays call 'al fresco dining', which means to eat in the wind while getting sunburnt.

buying

500 g (1 lb 2 oz) spaghettini
60 ml (¹/₄ cup) olive oil
500 g (1 lb 2 oz) pipis
2 garlic cloves, pasted (see tips, page 35)
2 small red chillies, deseeded and finely chopped
2 teaspoons lemon zest
3 tablespoons lemon juice
1–2 teaspoons sea salt
freshly ground black pepper
a handful of flat-leaf (Italian) parsley, chopped

cooking

Get a big saucepan of water on the go for the spag. When it's boiling, add some cooking salt and the pasta. Stir it around and cook for about 8 minutes, or until the pasta is al dente.

Get a big frying pan (with a lid) on the go for the pipis. When the pan is hot, add the oil and then the pipis. Toss them around and put the lid on. Keep the heat high. After a few minutes the pipis will have opened. Remove the lid, add the garlic, chilli and lemon zest. Toss everything around. Drain the pasta, reserving a couple of tablespoons of the cooking water, and return the pasta to its saucepan. Tip in the pipis and add the lemon juice. If the finished dish is a little dry, add a few tablespoons of pasta water. Plate. Salt, pepper, parsley. Serves 4

drinking

Dry, lightly bodied chardonnay or dry pinot grigio is good here. Or dry white blends from Western Australia. Marsanne is another good option, but stay away from riesling and sauvignon blanc — neither has the weight to match the carbo heft of the spag.

tips+tricks+tabletalk

Pipis can sometimes contain a little bit of sand — they're a bivalve, after all, and that's what they do for a living: suck in and spit out sandy water. Good fishmongers will sell only clean ones.

Cook your pipis on the day you buy them: no one likes a fishy pipi.

sunday tortilla

pipi spaghetti

Paella is a controversial dish. Food anthropologists will tell you that the stuff we all know as paella is actually not: it's *arroz a la marinera* (rice with seafood). It's just cooked in a paella pan. Real paella doesn't have fish in it — it's got chicken and rabbit and it's cooked over an outdoor wood fire. This dish is called *para bailar*, which means 'for dancing'. If you've got enough wine, these sorts of illegal paella lunches tend to degenerate into parties.

buying

1.5 litres (6 cups) chicken stock, preferably homemade
1 tablespoon olive oil
1 large onion, diced
2 garlic cloves, finely chopped
2 pinches of saffron threads
1 teaspoon paprika
1 squid tube, chopped into rings
3 ripe Roma (plum) tomatoes, roughly chopped
500 g (2 1/4 cups) good Italian arborio rice, or the Spanish stuff, if you can get it
300–400 g (10 1/2–14 oz) boneless white fish, such as bream, chopped into rough chunks
300–400 g (10 1/2–14 oz) blue eye cod, chopped into rough chunks
200 g (7 oz) raw king prawns (shrimp), peeled and deveined
1 lemon, cut into wedges

cooking

Put the chicken stock in a saucepan and bring to a simmer. Put the lid on and keep at a simmer.

If you don't have an authentic paella pan, use a large high-sided frying pan with a lid. Tip your olive oil in and, when it's hot, add the onion. When the onion is transparent, throw in the garlic, saffron, paprika and the squid. Stir all this together. Follow that up with the tomatoes. Now add the rice, stirring around briskly for 1 minute to coat all the grains with the juices in the pan.

Slowly add 1 litre (4 cups) of the simmering chicken stock, a ladleful at a time, stirring well after each addition. Add a large pinch of salt. Stir around, set your pan to a simmer and cook for about 10 minutes. Put in the two types of fish. Add more chicken stock as the rice absorbs the liquid. Keep checking the rice — it will probably take another 5–10 minutes — you want it just cooked. When it's ready, add the prawns and put the lid on. 2 more minutes. Serve with plenty of squeezed lemon and crusty bread. Tuck in. ¡Olé! Serves 4

drinking

If ever there was a dish designed for the consumption of rosé, it's this. Rosé is both a white wine that is a red wine and a red wine that is a white wine. And this is a fish dish that isn't. Choose a rosé that isn't too sweet or fruity — something with plenty of acidity and from a cool-climate wine region — and serve it cold. If you want to drink red, the chicken stock and earthiness of the saffron makes that a possibility. Nothing too stridently flavoured, oaky or poncy — understated earthy reds seem to go best.

tips+tricks+tabletalk

The utensil called a paella is a round, wide shallow receptacle made of metal. It's got two handles and a depth of about 4–7 cm (1 1/2–2 3/4 inches). They come in all sizes, some so large they're stirred with shovels and feed thousands of people.

You can modify this paella by changing the types of fish you use. Substituting Spanish mackerel for blue eye will make it more fishy. Adding mussels, likewise. Using ling or ocean perch will just make it boring.

This is one of those Spanish-inspired creations that is a meal in itself, while still leaving room for a salad and the all-important cheese course. It's a great illegal lunch because later on you'll still feel like a T-bone for dinner.

choriz o'chickpea

buying

2 tablespoons olive oil
2 chorizo sausages, chopped into discs about 5 mm (1/4 inch) wide — the thickness is up to you
8 saffron strands
2 x 300 g (10 1/2 oz) tins of chickpeas, drained
2 garlic cloves, pasted (see tips, page 35)
1 small fennel bulb or 1/3 of a large one, roughly diced
1 celery stalk, finely diced
1 red capsicum (pepper), membrane and seeds removed, chopped into fine rings
1 tablespoon sherry vinegar
250 ml (1 cup) dry white wine
250 ml (1 cup) tomato juice
3 tablespoons roughly chopped flat-leaf (Italian) parsley

99

cooking

Find a large lidded frying pan and put it (minus the lid) on high heat. Add the olive oil, swirl it around and then throw in the chorizo. Brown the sausage discs well for 3–5 minutes, or until they've taken on plenty of colour. Add the saffron, stir it around a bit and throw in the drained chickpeas. One more stir, then quickly add the garlic and all the vegetables. Follow that up with the sherry vinegar, then the white wine and, finally, the tomato juice.

Bring it up to a steady bubble, then reduce to a simmer, put the lid on and cook very gently for 15–20 minutes. If at any stage the pan gets too dry, add a few tablespoons of water. Once cooked, place in a warmed bowl and garnish with parsley. Serve with crusty bread. Serves 4

drinking

As this is quite a Spanish dish it's no surprise that red wines made in an Española style suit it. So buy tempranillo, Rioja, and the like. Or Spainitize your Australian shiraz cabernets by letting them air before you drink them (open them at 9 a.m.). A tiny bit of oxidization works wonders and can make a really anal Aussie red taste quite stylishly European.

Contrary to popular belief, the flavour in food is not just the result of ingredients, cooking, or the wine it is consumed with. Weather has a significant influence. Some weather conditions are just wrong for certain foods. Our research has shown that roasted meats taste best at relatively low barometric pressures; barbecued steak seems to be most tender when cooked slap bang in the middle of a slow-moving high-pressure system; fresh fish should be cooked under a light scattering of stratocumulus; and Sunny Pork Vermicelli is a dish best consumed on the last hot day before the cool change hits, when the barometer is falling and the cloud is building to the south. Or north, depending on which hemisphere you're in.

buying

1 thumb of ginger, grated
1 tablespoon soy sauce, plus extra to season
2 garlic cloves, pasted (see tips, page 35)
1 teaspoon olive oil, plus extra for stir-frying
400 g (14 oz) lean pork, finely sliced
250 g (9 oz) bean thread vermicelli
juice of 1 lemon
2 tablespoons sambal oelek (see tips)
1 Lebanese (short) cucumber, finely chopped
a small handful of coriander (cilantro) leaves, finely chopped
ditto of mint leaves, finely chopped
1 small red chilli, deseeded and finely chopped
a few whole coriander (cilantro) and mint leaves, to garnish

cooking

Make up a marinade of the ginger, soy sauce, garlic and olive oil. Add the pork and soak in the mixture for an hour or so.

Cook the vermicelli in boiling water for 3 minutes, or until just done. Drain and cool with cold water. Combine the lemon juice and sambal oelek in a small saucepan and bring to the boil.

Now put your wok or frying pan over high heat and add a splash of oil. Bounce and flip the pork slices around in the wok a couple of times and then take them out — they will continue to cook for a bit afterwards. Put the noodles in a large bowl with the sambal mixture, the cucumber, coriander, mint and chilli. Toss it all together. Add the pork, garnish with the coriander and mint leaves and serve. Season with soy sauce but go easy on this. Serves 4

drinking

This luncheon dish seems to rise a few notches when served with a heavily chilled, unctuous dry white. That word 'unctuous' means that varieties such as riesling and sauvignon blanc won't have what it takes, but grapes such as pinot grigio and viognier will. Both of the latter have the capacity to be fresh tasting but with a more glycerol texture than most whites.

tips+tricks+tabletalk

Sambal oelek is an Indonesian salty spicy paste made from ground chillies. It is available from Asian food stores and some supermarkets.

sunny pork vermicelli

artichoke, asparagus, broad beans and peas

artichoke, asparagus, broad beans and peas

104

A healthful and uplifting lunch, AABBP also doubles as a fairly poncy first course, particularly if you've just bought a new home and you are rubbing in the fact by constantly inviting old friends around for dinner parties. This recipe can also be a platform from which you can build a lot of salads, pastas or vegetable stews. Just make sure you always add a bit of bacon, otherwise people will be calling you a #*$% vegetarian.

buying

1 rasher of bacon, finely chopped
12 asparagus spears
3 globe artichokes
600 g (1 lb 5 oz) fresh broad (fava) beans, podded
250 g (9 oz) fresh peas, podded (125 g/4 1/2 oz
   shelled weight)
100 g (3 1/2 oz) feta cheese, crumbled
sea salt and freshly ground black pepper
2 tablespoons chopped mint

dressing:
1/2 teaspoon balsamic vinegar
1/2 teaspoon Dijon mustard
1/2 teaspoon lemon juice
2 tablespoons la de dah olive oil

cooking

Fry the chopped bacon in a hot frying pan until crispy. Set aside. Bring a large saucepan of water to a rolling boil.

Snap the woody stems off the asparagus. Pull three layers of leaves from each artichoke and trim off the top one-third of the artichoke flower. Cut off the bottom one-third of the artichoke's stem. Using a paring knife or vegetable peeler, trim the artichoke, removing the rough, fibrous outer layers of the leaf base and stem skin. Chop the artichoke into quarters, down the stem. Using the paring knife or a small knife, chop out and discard the fluffy, fibrous heart of the choke — it'll be easy to do now that you're only tackling a quarter of the artichoke at a time.

Throw the artichoke quarters, the broad beans and the peas into the saucepan of water, along with a dash of salt. Cook for 7 minutes, then add the asparagus. Cook for 1 more minute after the water returns to the boil. Drain all the vegetables and refresh them for 2 minutes in a sink full of cold water and ice cubes. Drain.

Now the dressing. In a large stainless-steel bowl, pour in the balsamic, mustard and lemon juice. Whisk this about until it has amalgamated, then add the olive oil and whisk again. Tip in the drained vegies, the feta and bacon and arrange this mess in an avant-garde style on a rustic-looking plate. Salt and pepper. Sprinkle with mint. Serves 4

drinking

Artichokes ruin all good wine. Or that's one wine theory. Nonsense! This vegie salad is tailor-made for semillon/ sauvignon blanc blends. The sauvignon blanc component will take care of the asparagus, as well as the artichoke.

tips+tricks+tabletalk

This same recipe tossed through pasta will feed a football team. You could toss in slices of fried sausage instead of the bacon.
You can serve this dish either warm, at room temperature or cold.

carne d'lazy

This is the only time you'll ever catch us endorsing that otherwise useless piece of meat known as beef fillet. This recipe does have something else to recommend it, however: you get to use a hammer.

buying

250 g (9 oz) beef eye fillet
2 handfuls of rocket (arugula) leaves, washed and spun dry
4 tablespoons of the best extra virgin olive oil you can find
1¹/₂ tablespoons balsamic vinegar
sea salt and freshly ground black pepper
1 lemon, halved
a small piece of Parmigiano Reggiano cheese, about 70 g (2¹/₂ oz)

cooking

Put the beef in the freezer for 10 minutes while you assemble the other ingredients, and wash and dry the rocket.

Then, using your sharpest knife, slice the beef into eight very, very thin steaks. Put each slice in between two layers of plastic — a clean, recycled clear plastic bag is good for this. Pick up the hammer and, tapping not too forcefully, start thinning out the beef, working from the centre of the piece towards the edges. If you can't triple the area of the beef by this process you are not trying hard enough. You want the beef to be opaque, but still holding together. Repeat this with the other slices, then lay them out on four plates, two to a plate.

Plonk some rocket to one side of the plate and dress everything with the combined olive oil, balsamic vinegar and salt and pepper. Before serving, squeeze some lemon juice over the top and shave the cheese on with a vegetable peeler. Serves 4

drinking

Dry, minerally, savoury red wine is great with this. Whatever you do, steer clear of any red with too much oak. You're looking for counterpoint here. Barbera is a good choice; its slight acidity is like an extra squeeze of lemon. Failing that, choose lean, minimally oaked shiraz from cool climates.

tips+tricks+tabletalk

Rubbing the plates with some garlic before adding the meat isn't a bad idea.

To make a slight variation on the dressing for the rocket (arugula) and meat, add a bit of mustard and horseradish to the olive oil and balsamic vinegar.

dead thin

dead things on toast

'Hors d'oeuvres must be presented elegantly. The lady of the house must not only supervise their presentation, but must co-operate in it and put herself out to devise original and graceful decorative effects.'

Larousse Gastronomique, Prosper Montagne (Editor)

Dead things on toast, crustaceans on crackers, bivalves on bickies, canapés, hors d'oeuvres, tapas, antipasto, appetizers, pre-prandials... There are many names in many languages for this non-meal but the purpose is the same. Ergonomically designed so that you can hold them in one hand while the other is wrapped around a glass, these are comestibles with flavours that are piquant, savoury and incomplete without an accompanying beverage. Dainty bites of these little foodstuffs and sips of aperitif wines are like the warm-up exercises that an athlete does before a big event — the only difference is that your event is dinner.

The appetizer hour ('beer o'clock' in some cultures) is also an occasion when the food and the wine hold equal billing. Take either away and it's just not the same. The whole is greater than the sum of the parts. A fresh appetite and a clean palate appreciate the synergy of food and wine more than at any other time. Our subconscious balances those first sharp tastes of alcohol with the food at hand. The way the saltiness of an olive soothes the acidity of that first sip of wine. How the bitterness of a beer seems to make a packet of salty chips taste fantastic.

At this time of day, unless you're unwell, the appetite needs no stimulation. Hungry people with their first drink in hand don't need to be cajoled into eating, and anything remotely edible will be devoured. But this is a sacred moment. Virginal appetites are precious things and should not be squandered on a handful of nuts.

Contrary to what many glossy food magazines would suggest, the most important ingredient needed at this time is not smoked salmon, crabmeat or pheasant pâté — it is imagination. The challenge is to turn what you have available into a memorable tidbit. A quick stocktake of fridge and cupboard; some frenzied, inspired kitchen activity; some good wine: the job's sorted. That's what the recipes in this chapter are about. Recycling, re-inventing, and revving things up a little bit before the main event.

petits gateaux de poisson

We could crap on about how this dish is a French-slash-Vietnamese version of Thai fish cake that we discovered in Old Hanoi during last year's fish cake discovery tour, but it's not. We just like the French translation. This is our version of the fish cakes at our local Thai restaurant.

buying

113

600 g (1 lb 5 oz) red fish (nannygai) fillets, skinned and boned
2 garlic cloves
2 egg whites
a handful of mint leaves
2 small red chillies
a handful of coriander (cilantro) leaves
500 ml (2 cups) olive oil
Thai chilli sauce, for dipping

cooking

Blend all the ingredients, except the oil and chilli sauce, in a food processor. Shape the petits gateaux in the palm of your hand and roll them into a plump cigarish shape. (Cigar-shaped fish cakes are easier and more elegant to eat with the fingers.) Set aside.

Heat the oil in a wok until it is just on the verge of smoking. Put in the fish cakes three at a time and fry until golden brown. Drain on paper towels and serve with Thai chilli sauce. Serves 4

drinking

We've tasted just about every wine known to man with these petits gateaux and the wine that comes out best every time is riesling and, more specifically, Tasmanian riesling. Riesling from that great state tends to be finer, more austere and more delicately flavoured than many other Australian rieslings. The lemon and lime flavours suit the fish and fight the chilli sauce.

Red fish, or nannygai, is the best fish. It's cheap, easy to get and the soft sweet flesh works especially well with the aforesaid Tasmanian riesling. Other fish that could be substituted are bream or very, very fresh blackfish (luderick).

If you like your fish cakes really fluffy, add another egg white.

Squid, or calamari, can seem to some people a pretty ugly, slimy and daunting food item, particularly in its raw state. Where's the head? Which bit do I eat? Will it squirt ink at me? Will it taste like a rubber band? Muster some courage, or have a couple of glasses of white, and tackle a calamari or two. You'll feel like a real man — even if you're a woman. Don't be frightened — it's dead. Squidette is perfect drinks party food because it comes in little bits, it's got plenty of flavour and it's great with white wine or beer. And the sight of you nonchalantly and quickly preparing and cooking this in your bedsit will impress the guests no end.

squidette

buying

1 medium-sized squid, about 250 g (9 oz)
40 g (1/3 cup) plain (all-purpose) flour
1 teaspoon salt
1 teaspoon freshly ground black pepper
4–6 tablespoons olive oil
1 lemon

cooking

The first thing is to keep the paper and the plastic bag the squid came in — use the plastic bag for all the yukky bits you'll need to chuck out. To prepare the squid, gently pull the tentacles and the head out of the body. Cut the head from the tentacles just below the squid's mouth or beak (if you can make that out), chuck out the head and then cut the tentacles into single appendages.

Pull out the guts and the bony stem (the thing that looks like a piece of plastic) from the body or tube. Using your hands, strip the outer black and grey skin from the body and pull off the two wings. Strip the skin off them as well and also cut away the thin line of cartilage that runs along the wing's broken side. Cut along the seam inside and flatten out the tube. It will be triangular in shape. Tear off any glucky bits from the inside and then cut the body in half lengthways. Including the two wings, you'll have four triangular bits of squid. Chop those four bits into small bite-sized strips — about the size of a clothes peg.

Lay out the paper the squid was wrapped in and put the flour, salt and pepper onto it. Add the squid pieces and tentacles and coat in the flour by rolling them around through the salt and pepper mixture. Remove the squid, shaking off the excess flour, then tip away the flour and recycle the paper once more for absorbing the oil when frying the squid.

Heat 2–3 tablespoons of the oil in a really hot non-stick frying pan — you've got to get your oil absolutely smoking. Add half the squid, but don't crowd the pan, and fry it flat chat. Turn it all after 30 seconds and watch out because it spits and spatters and jumps around, especially if it's really fresh. Cook for another 1 1/2 minutes, then remove the squid with tongs or a slotted spoon and let them drain on the paper. Add the remaining oil and do the other batch. More salt and pepper if you need it, lots of lemon juice and turn up the music to drown out the smoke alarm. Serves 4

drinking

The texture of the squid and the weight of flavour provided by the oil and the flour make this a good bet with well-chilled chardonnay. Adding a little bit more salt to the mixture makes it taste really good with a crisp hoppy lager.

cheat's pizza

This pizza is quick, versatile, very good for drunk people and ideal with whatever wine is left. Besides the ingredients, you only need two things: a very hot oven and a bit of flair. You can fake the latter, but not the former.

buying

1 round of Greek or Middle Eastern pitta bread
1 heaped tablespoon tomato paste (purée)
1 tablespoon pesto
1 rasher of bacon, rind removed, finely chopped
6 olives, pitted and ripped up into little bits
some fresh herbs, roughly chopped
4 bocconcini, ripped up
olive oil, to drizzle

cooking

Turn your oven to its highest setting. If you've got a fan-forced oven, ditto. Let it warm up for 20 minutes. Put the round of bread on a pizza tray. Now spread the tomato paste and the pesto over this fake pizza base. Sprinkle over all the other ingredients and distribute them evenly. Scantly drizzle some olive oil over everything. But, remember, scantly.

Pop into the oven for 10 minutes — it might take more or less, depending on the oven's upper limit. You want the topping browned but the base still a little doughy. And depending on how drunk you all are, you might need to cook the whole packet of pitta bread.
Serves 1

116

drinking

Everything, from beer to white to red to sparkler. Maybe not rum. Cheap red wine that is not too toxic works best.

A range of toppings works with this, just don't overload the base too much: anchovy, leftover vegetables, a bit of chilli, very finely sliced red capsicum (pepper), red onion, feta cheese or mushrooms. The bacon can be substituted with any other processed meat: salami, ham or finely chopped leftover sausages.

sang choy mao

Word has it that this is what Chairman Mao enjoyed on the Long March. There was no cos lettuce on the way to Peking — that's one of the ingredients we've substituted, as well as pork for the roadside fauna — bats, beetles, lizards…

buying

4 pork spare ribs, rind removed, bone cut out
2 garlic cloves, roughly chopped
a thumb of ginger, roughly chopped
85 g (3 oz) block of dried wheat noodles
1 tablespoon olive oil
4 large button mushrooms, very finely diced
4 spring onions (scallions), finely sliced
125 ml (1/2 cup) riesling
2 tablespoons light soy sauce, plus extra to serve
125 ml (1/2 cup) chicken stock
90 g (1 cup) bean sprouts
2 tablespoons finely chopped coriander (cilantro) leaves
1 cos (romaine) lettuce, broken into individual leaves

cooking

Finely mince the meat from your spare ribs (ribs are cheaper and have a better flavour than minced pork), along with the garlic and ginger in a mincer or food processor. Then take your noodles, put them in a tough plastic bag and bash them until they're broken.

Put the olive oil into a hot wok and add the minced ingredients. Stir and toss this around until it has taken on a nice dark brown colour. Add the mushrooms and spring onions. Then add the liquid in the following order, stirring once between each addition: wine, soy sauce, chicken stock. Immediately add the broken noodles and mix thoroughly. Low heat. Cover and cook for 10 minutes — adjust with a tablespoon of water if the mixture becomes too dry. Add the bean sprouts and coriander and remove from the heat. Cool for 10 minutes.

OK. Load each lettuce leaf with some meat mixture, using the leaves from the heart first. The tiny inner leaves of the cos serve well as finger food vehicles; use the bigger leaves for entrée-sized serves. Serve with the extra soy sauce. Serves 4

drinking

Go for a limey, yet fairly rich riesling with this dish. Stick to cooler climates and a reasonably recent vintage. Or throw some smashed up unsalted peanuts into the Mao at the end of cooking and serve cheap chardy instead.

tempura
The Portuguese introduced tempura to Japan about 400 years ago. The key to tempura is quick service: slice, batter, fry, eat. Japanese tempura masters reckon that the perfect batter is like a revealing dress.

buying

120

100 g (3 1/2 oz) plain (all-purpose) flour
170 ml (2/3 cup) soda water
about 750 ml (3 cups) olive oil or vegetable oil
a range of vegetables — broccoli, zucchini (courgettes), beans,
    capsicums (peppers), fine slices of ginger, mushrooms, asparagus
    — sliced into a range of shapes, none bigger than a cork
a dash of sesame oil, if that's your thing
sea salt
2 lemons

cooking

Put the flour in a large stainless-steel bowl and add the soda water slowly, beating the mixture gently until the flour is just incorporated. Do not beat out all the lumps. Let the batter stand for 30 minutes.

Pour the oil into a wok. Turn the heat to high. You will have to experiment a little with the temperature of the oil. Frying points for different types of oils vary. Olive oil has a stronger flavour than vegetable oil, but it has a higher smoking threshold. In other words, it is harder to burn things in it. A splash of sesame oil in with the main oil component is a good trick — add just a dash for flavour.

When the oil starts to shimmer and smoke, dredge your vegetables in the batter, drain off the excess and drop into the wok. Fry six pieces at a time. 1 minute is all it will take. Drain on paper towels or some old butcher's paper, if you've got some. Salt and lemon juice. Get a production line going and keep cooking and eating the tempura around the kitchen bench. There are always people in the kitchen at parties... Serves 4

drinking

The oiliness of the tempura requires acidity and zing. That's why God made sauvignon blanc. Serve it as close to freezing as you can. Or if you have really poncy wine addicts in attendance, serve bone-dry riesling. Riesling is the world's greatest white wine. It is white wine in its purest form — unoaked and unadorned.

holy trinity tapenade

This is so-called because it contains The Father, The Son and The Holy Ghost of the appetizer hour: olives, capers and anchovies. It's as salty as Lake Eyre, which makes it an excellent vehicle with most drinks. Why? It's simple. Eat tapenade. Get thirsty. Drink. Eat tapenade. Get thirsty. Drink...

buying

100 g (2/3 cup) pitted Kalamata olives
2 tablespoons salted capers, rinsed
2 anchovy fillets
2 tablespoons olive oil
1 large handful of flat-leaf (Italian) parsley
2 tablespoons fino sherry (optional)

cooking

Throw everything in the food processor and whizz. Go for a roughly puréed but not-too-smooth texture. Adjust the consistency with the olive oil and serve on biscuits, bread or bits of cold boiled potato. This is best made about 1 hour ahead to allow all the flavours to develop. Serves 4

drinking

It will be a long time before they're serving tapenade with the tap beer at unreconstructed pubs. It's a shame because they go really well together — much better than chips flavoured with fake chicken dust. So beer and, more specifically, cold hoppy lager. Or young white wine, such as unwooded semillon. Cold Spanish fino sherry is an absolute winner too, especially when you add it to the tapenade.

tips+tricks+tabletalk

Little Kalamatas have a better flavour than the larger ones. It takes more time to take out the stones but it's worth it.

You can tweak the saltiness by adding or subtracting anchovies. But don't overdo them.

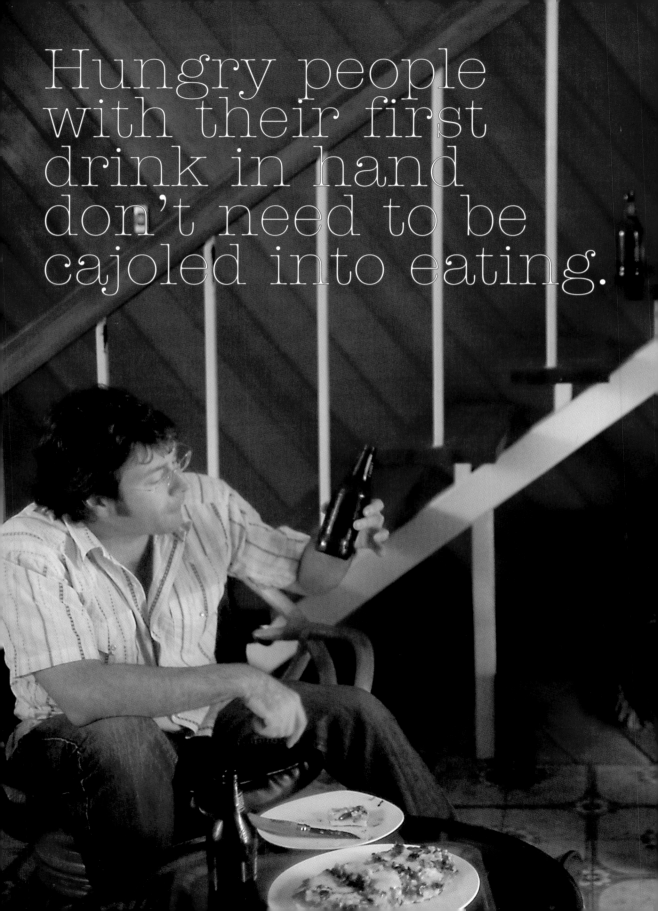

Hungry people with their first drink in hand don't need to be cajoled into eating.

sweetness' dumplings

This recipe was developed by 'Sweetness', Greg's beloved. The dumplings are filled with silverbeet, but almost anything can be whizzed up and gow geed — try pork, prawn or chicken.

buying

1 medium bunch of silverbeet (Swiss chard)
90 g (3 1/4 oz) tin of water chestnuts, drained
2 tablespoons soy sauce, plus extra to serve
1 egg white
3 tablespoons cornflour (cornstarch)
1 teaspoon sake or rice wine vinegar
2 garlic cloves
1 red chilli
275 g (9 3/4 oz) packet of fresh gow gee or won ton wrappers
    (gow gee wrappers give the best texture)
wasabi, to serve

cooking

Wash the silverbeet and cut away the white stems. Pat the leaves really dry. Put all the ingredients, except the wrappers, into a food processor with salt and pepper and whizz until nearly smooth.

Lay the gow gee wrappers on a board. Put a teaspoon of the silverbeet mixture into the centre of each wrapper and, using water and your index finger, moisten the edges of each wrapper so that they stick firmly together when folded. Fold the wrapper over the filling to make a semicircle, then press down the edges with a fork. This all sounds complicated but you'll soon work it out.

Heat a large saucepan of salted water and gently drop in the dumplings. Bring back to the boil and simmer gently for about 4 minutes. Drain. Mix a dab of wasabi into some soy to make a dipping sauce for the gow gees. Serves 4

drinking

The saltiness of the soy sauce and the slippery boiled gow gees mean that the best drink is beer: hoppy Asian brews such as Tsingtao, Singha and Kirin are especially good. If you must drink wine, low-alcohol, fairly neutral-tasting whites, such as unwooded semillon, are good. Chinese tea isn't bad either.

antipasto donna

Antipasto means 'before the meal'. It can also mean 'ruining your appetite'. Dead things on toast have lots of different names: hors d'oeuvres, tapas, mezze or zakuski. But if you're going to be molto Italiano, here are a few vegies to enliven your pre-dinner platters.

buying

125

1 red capsicum (pepper)
8 asparagus spears
12 button mushrooms, halved
2 zucchinis (courgettes), sliced lengthways into 4 or 5 strips
1 small eggplant (aubergine), sliced lengthways into 5 mm (1/4 inch) slices
juice of 1 lemon
125 ml (1/2 cup) olive oil
60 ml (1/4 cup) balsamic vinegar
1 small red chilli, finely chopped

cooking

Put the whole capsicum directly over the flame of a gas jet and singe it all over for a few minutes (or do this under your griller/broiler). Once blackened, pop it in a plastic bag and seal it up. Leave this to one side. Snap off and discard the woody stems of the asparagus. Drop the edible spear ends into a saucepan of boiling water for 1 minute, then refresh in cold water. Throw the mushrooms, zucchini and eggplant into a bowl, and mix in the lemon juice, oil, balsamic vinegar and chilli.

Heat a barbecue grill or chargrill pan over medium heat. Remove the vegetables from the marinade (reserve the marinade) and the asparagus from the water and cook them until you achieve some el scorchio-ed effects.

Meanwhile, remove the capsicum from the plastic bag and peel off the blackened skin, cut out the membrane and remove the seeds. Slice the flesh into strips and add to the reserved marinade along with the grilled vegetables. Leave to stand for 1 hour before transforming them into a stunning antipasto platter. Serves 4

drinking

Young riesling. Choose fruitier rieslings from Victoria. Young semillon is another good option. If you do go for red, such as a cheapy Italian sangiovese, make sure you've got some lumps of Parmigiano and slices of prosciutto or mortadella also on the plate.

meatballs

Another late-at-night, everyone's-drunk-quick-I-better-feed-them recipe. Always keep a quarter of a kilo of mince in the freezer, have a microwave set to 'defrost', and always have a bottle of tomato sauce and a tin of anchovies in the cupboard. And always — ALWAYS — have one more bottle of red wine hidden somewhere.

buying

250 g (9 oz) minced (ground) beef, or a veal/pork mix
1 teaspoon plain (all-purpose) flour
20 g (³/4 oz) tinned anchovies (about 5–6 fillets)
1 tablespoon tomato paste (purée)
a knob of butter
1 tablespoon olive oil
a dash of red wine vinegar

cooking

If it's frozen, defrost the mince. A bit obvious, we know, but this is a recipe book. Use your hands and squish the mince, flour, anchovies and tomato paste together. A bowl is handy. Fashion the goo into little balls — the smaller the better.

Heat the butter and a splash of olive oil in a non-stick pan and slowly brown the meatballs. Medium to low heat for 8–10 minutes. Take your time. Add a dash of red wine vinegar to the pan towards the end of the frying to add some much needed piquancy to your balls. Serve with tomato sauce for dipping. Serves 4

drinking

As with most late night drinking sessions or suppers, you invariably drink your best, most loved and prized wine. It's Bacchus' way of telling you to get over yourself and be less serious about wine. That's why expensive cabernet is perfect with these meatballs — the best one you have.

tips+tricks+tabletalk

Add any of the following ingredients to the meatball matrix: fresh herbs, finely chopped bacon, mushroom, a dash of soy sauce, Worcestershire sauce or an egg, for protein's sake.

Use tinned anchovies and not the ones in jars, as the latter get light-struck and lose their flavour quickly.

fushi

This is the ideal fish dish for blackouts, when the gas bottle has run out, or if it's really hot and you don't want any more heat in the kitchen. We've christened it Fushi — pronounced not like sushi but the same way New Zealanders pronounce fish — because the template for this recipe came from a wine-tasting junket to New Zealand.

buying

128

1 garlic clove, halved
125 ml (1/2 cup) fresh lemon juice
2 tablespoons olive oil
1 large ripe avocado, diced
400 g (14 oz) very good quality, fresh (preferably sashimi-grade) boneless blue fin tuna, diced
4 tablespoons chopped basil
250 g (9 oz) punnet of cherry tomatoes, halved
slices of toasted rye bread, to serve
sea salt and freshly ground black pepper

cooking

Rub a bowl with the halved garlic clove, then add the lemon juice, oil, avocado and tuna. Mix in the basil and tomatoes, then refrigerate for 10 minutes or so. During this time the lemon juice will partially 'cook' the fish. Serve on thin slices of toasted rye bread. Generously sprinkle with salt and pepper. Serves 4

drinking

Fushi will taste pretty good with most whites, but good quality New Zealand sauvignon blanc is the most worthy juice. It's just as powerful as the Fushi, but they don't seem to fight for palate dominance. Alternatively, well-chilled Western Australian semillon/sauvignon blends are a good choice.

Other fish can be used in place of blue fin, as long as it's very good quality, fresh, boneless and not too chewy. Salmon and snapper are good but, as with all partly raw fish dishes, freshness is critical. Otherwise it will taste…well…fishy.

grao-de-bicos

The Portuguese never waste anything, and make everything go with wine or coffee or whatever they're drinking. It's not fancy, it's not fine and it doesn't photograph particularly well, but it is always very tasty. This very basic bar food is something Greg picked up on a working holiday in Portugal.

buying

250 g (9 oz) packet of good quality dried chickpeas
5 garlic cloves, sliced into little chips
2 tablespoons good olive oil
a handful of finely chopped coriander (cilantro) leaves
good sea salt

cooking

First soak your chickpeas for yonks — overnight or at least half a day, discarding any loose skins. Boil them in plenty of water and when they are very tender, drain them and set aside.

Fry the garlic chips in the oil until they just start to go golden, being careful not to burn them. When they've achieved the right colour, turn off the heat, get them out with a slotted spoon and discard them. Tip the chickpeas into your serving bowl, pour over the garlic-infused oil and stick in the fridge until everything cools down to room temperature. Toss in your chopped coriander, add plenty of sea salt and serve. Serves 4

130

drinking

This is bar food, so it goes with just about anything that comes from a bar, except Tia Maria, Baileys Irish Cream and those sorts of toxic liquors. It's best with really cold fino sherry, tangy pale ales and dry rosés.

You may think that coriander (cilantro) is a pretty weird sort of herb to use here but coriander, or *coentro* as the Portuguese call it, is the single most widely used herb in Portugal. It's available all year round and they use it in everything, and especially with garlic.

Our motto is, 'Don't let the bin eat something that you still can'. This is a recipe perfect for those bits of old cheese that end up in some forgotten compartment of the fridge. The Cheddar that's gone furry, the scary Stilton, the ammoniacal Camembert and the Brie can all find an edible home in the cheesy pouf.

cheesy poufs

buying

125 g (1 cup) old cheese, grated, mushed, poured or crumbled into bits
125 g (1 cup) plain (all-purpose) flour
2 teaspoons baking powder
a pinch of rock salt
1 egg
100 ml (3 1/2 fl oz) milk
1 small onion, grated
4 tablespoons chopped flat-leaf (Italian) parsley

131

cooking

Preheat the oven to 200°C (400°F/Gas 6). Mix the cheese, flour, baking powder and salt in a bowl. Break the egg into a teacup, beat lightly with a fork and top up with the milk. Fold this through the dry ingredients along with the onion and parsley. Drop spoonfuls of the mixture into well-greased gem irons and bake for 10–15 minutes. If you don't have gem irons, non-stick biscuit trays are also good. In this case, the size and shape of the poufs will depend on what you cook them in. Best served hot. Serves 4

drinking

This depends very much on the cheese you use. If you've gone for the runny Camembert, a chilled lager is good. But if you've included a blue cheese at the end of its edible life, the cheesy pouf is one of the few things that goes well with sparkling red wine. For standard Cheddar, the drink of choice is Australian sparkling white.

tips+tricks+tabletalk

Old cheesy poufs can be made to appear 'oven fresh' by smearing their tops with a dab of butter and giving them a zazz in the microwave for 30 seconds or so.

This recipe can be tweaked with herbs. Throw in some basil for freshness or some chives for extra bite.

sushi in the hand

To appear edible, raw fish has to look pretty. Have you ever seen a fisherman eat his catch straight off the hook? Until they're resting on their little couch of rice, bits of raw fish are not that appealing — unless you're a seal.

buying

200 g (1 cup) Japanese short-grain rice
125 ml (1/2 cup) rice vinegar
1 tablespoon sugar
wasabi
250 g (9 oz) sashimi-grade tuna
light soy sauce, to serve

133

cooking

Boil your rice until soft but not gluggy, drain very well in a colander, then transfer to a shallow dish. Meanwhile, heat 80 ml (1/3 cup) of the vinegar with the sugar and 2 good pinches of salt in a saucepan until the sugar dissolves. Whatever you do, don't boil it. Pour the vinegar mixture over the back of a spoon onto the rice. Using a flat-bladed knife, 'cut' the mixture into the rice to spread it around. Leave the rice to cool to room temperature.

Pour the remaining vinegar into a bowl of water. Dip your hands in this to prevent the rice sticking to them, then take a small handful of rice and mould and roll it into an oblong about 5 cm (2 inches) long. This takes a bit of practice, but you'll get the hang of it. Put a tiny dob of wasabi on each oblong of rice.

To make your sushi, take a squarely cut piece of tuna. Using a very sharp knife, cut 5 mm (1/4 inch) diagonal slices off the tuna, holding the knife at a 45 degree angle. Clean up any daggy bits on each slice, then press the tuna on top of the rice oblongs. Serve with a dipping mixture made from soy sauce with a bit of wasabi mixed through it. Serves 4 (makes 12)

drinking

Fine, delicate aromatic white wines are the only choice here. Limey rieslings from South Australia's Clare and Eden Valleys are the best. Zingy sauvignon blancs from New Zealand are good too — if you like that sort of thing.

tips+tricks+tabletalk

The whack of wasabi is totally in your hands — or finger. What you dab onto the rice determines the heat. But it is better to use too little than too much — the flavours here should be delicate. Besides, you can always rev up the heat when applying the dipping mixture.

The best bit of the blue fin tuna for sushi comes from the belly. It's called oho toro, it's light pink in colour, marbled with fat and melts in the mouth.

fine dinin

fine dining, darling

'A maidservant brought water for him and poured it from a splendid golden pitcher, holding it above a silver basin for him to wash, and she pulled a polished table before him. A grave housekeeper brought in the bread and served it to him, adding many good things to it, generous in her provisions. Then long-suffering great Odysseus ate and drank.'

The Odyssey, Book VII, Homer

This is fine dining as it was after the fall of Troy, about 1500 BC. How much more civilized can it get? There are all the important things: wine, bread, lots of good things to eat, clean hands and a grave housekeeper — not some smart-arse sommelier. The post-modern dinner party, however, has become decadent: an opportunity for people to vaingloriously gloat, to show off their house, their possessions, their spouse, their cooking, their cellar, or all of the above. The simple beauty of eating with others (or, indeed, alone) has vanished up its own napery.

This is not what it's about. Over the years we have lost the true reason why people invite each other to their houses to eat. It's for companionship, repartee, wit, warmth, good food and good wine. In order to pull this off you need a spirit of generosity and an open mind. It doesn't matter if you are the host or the guest — both qualities are required. A social dinner is no place for egoism. When dinner parties become showdowns, with the return bout scheduled for the following Saturday, you know it's time to find a new circle of intimate friends/pugilists.

Kitchens were once the province of the matriarch. They cooked with fat and without ego. But in our bourgeois times the kitchen has become a magnet for all sorts of dreams, desires and needs. The control freak, especially, is attracted to a stove (particularly a Smeg) like a leech to a bushwalker. Obsessive-compulsive cooking inevitably follows. We know this because one of us has suffered this affliction (he's in remission now but still has to watch what he cooks).

Yet it is true that you can't invite people around for dinner and serve up three-bean mix out of a tin. A little bit of effort is involved — all the recipes in this chapter don't make themselves — but if you find yourself spending more time sautéing than socializing, flambéing than flirting, and drizzling, draining and dicing rather than drinking, you're becoming an obsessive-compulsive cook and you need help.

fruits de sea
Cute little curls of seafood creatively styled on a silver-rimmed, white dinner plate. Sauce. Sophistication.

buying

138

4 prawns (shrimp)
1 cutlet of blue eye cod, snapper, mackerel, kingfish or salmon
8 mussels
1 tablespoon olive oil
4 baby octopus, cleaned (and halved, if large)
1 garlic clove, partly squashed with the side of your knife
3 saffron threads
1 teaspoon butter
1/2 lemon
4 oysters
sea salt and freshly ground black pepper
a sprig of dill, to serve (optional)

cooking

Heat a small saucepan containing 250 ml (1 cup) water over medium heat. Remove the shells from the prawns but not their heads or tails. Throw the shells into the pot. Cut the four pockets of meat from the fish cutlet and throw the remnant bone and any fatty fish cuttings into the pot. Bring to the boil and simmer very gently — you now have fish stock.

Pull the beards from the mussels and give the shells a good scrub. Put a large frying pan on high heat. Add the mussels. Reduce the heat to medium. Cover the frying pan for a few minutes — when the mussels have opened, remove them from the pan. Add the oil to the pan and throw in the fish pieces, octopus, prawns, garlic and saffron. Medium heat. Cook, uncovered, for 3 minutes, turning once. Return the mussels to the pan and cook over low heat for 1–2 minutes until all the seafood is cooked. Remove all the fish to a warm plate.

Now, the sauce. The heat of your frying pan is critical here. If it is too hot before the stock goes in, the stock will instantly evaporate. Pour the fish stock into the pan, adjust the heat and reduce to a runny glaze. Stir through the butter and a squeeze of lemon juice. Arrange the cooked fish and the oysters evenly on four plates and drizzle on the sauce (not over the oysters). Salt, pepper, a sprig of fresh dill if you like. Serves 2, or 4 as an entrée

drinking

Chardonnay, and fairly posh stuff, is needed here. Anything made with French oak and showing some minerality: New Zealand, or Australian wines from Tasmania, South Australia, good stuff from the Hunter Valley or Victoria. Rich, spicy white wine flavours and a gamut of seafood textures — yum. $$$ white Burgundy would be even better.

Sometimes a recipe becomes a classic not because of anything particularly adventurous about its flavour or any fancy fusioning, but just because it really works. This one uses some of salmon's old friends: dill, lemon, salt and pepper. The way it's cooked and the way it's served make it an impressive entrée. You only need one salmon fillet (it goes a long way) and it's incredibly easy to make. There's the added ponce factor of double plating — that is, serving the salmon direct from the oven upon the plate on which it's cooked, then placing that plate upon another larger plate, so as not to burn your fine dining table. The effect — with correctly folded napery, fancy stemware and the bit of salmon sitting on the plate like a silk handkerchief — will send all but the most bitter food critic into a spin.

buying

300–400 g (10¹/₂–14 oz) very fresh, thick salmon fillet
4 teaspoons unsalted butter
sea salt and freshly ground black pepper
good quality olive oil
2 tablespoons roughly chopped dill
1 lemon, quartered

cooking

If you're game, remove the line of bones from the fish fillet with a pair of tweezers then, using a sharp knife, slice the skin off the fillet. Slice the raw fillet horizontally into four escalopes about 3–4 mm (¹/₈–¹/₄ inch) thick. Confidence is everything. Or get your fishmonger to do this for you.

Preheat the oven to 180°C (350°F/Gas 4). Take ¹/₂ teaspoon of the butter and smear it around the middle of an ovenproof side plate. Place one escalope of salmon on the plate — don't lay it flat but let it lie slightly creased and casual, much as a silk handkerchief would lie if you had carefully dropped it. Sprinkle with freshly ground salt and pepper and drop another ¹/₂ teaspoon of butter on top of the salmon. Drizzle the salmon very lightly with good olive oil. Repeat for the other three pieces of salmon.

Put the four plates into the oven for 4 minutes (a fan-forced oven will cook salmon evenly in this time but an older, more conventional oven might take 1–2 minutes longer). Once cooked — you want the salmon to be half pink, half opaque — sprinkle over some roughly chopped dill and a good squeeze of lemon. Serve atop bigger insulating dinner plates. Serves 4 as an entrée

drinking

Farmed salmon is a pretty rich, heavy and, for fish, a luxuriously (but harmlessly) fatty dish. You might think that a luxuriously rich wine like chardonnay would go with this. You'd be partly right, but you need a bit more cut and thrust. That's why a sparkling white wine — made from chardonnay in the *methode Champenoise* style — is the ticket. This adds even more class to your guests' fine dining experience. If you don't want to drink fizz, go for a really austere, tight chardonnay — something fancy from Tasmania or the Adelaide Hills, or that little-known French region called Chablis. There are some petits Chablis wines around that don't cost the world.

salmon on a plate

bunny stew

bunny stew

One of the great things about dinner parties is the opportunity they give you to serve your friends foods they claim not to like. If Ben had a dollar for every time he served his small circle of long-suffering friends bunny, goat, koala...

buying

1 rabbit, about 1.8 kg (4 lb)
3 tablespoons plain (all-purpose) flour
1 tablespoon olive oil
1 onion, halved (chop one half finely and the other half into
    four pieces)
2 garlic cloves, peeled and squashed
2 rashers of bacon, rind removed, chopped into rough strips
8 baby carrots, topped and tailed
mixed fresh herbs and a bay leaf
250 ml (1 cup) dry white wine
about 500 ml (2 cups) water or chicken stock

144

cooking

Preheat the oven to 150°C (300°F/Gas 2). Joint the rabbit into six pieces. Cut off the two back legs, cut its torso into two pieces and then cut the remaining upper body through the spine. Sprinkle these with plain flour.

Heat the olive oil in a stainless-steel saucepan over high heat. Add the rabbit in batches and get it well browned. This will take about 7–10 minutes. If things start to burn, lower the heat to medium. Remove the bunny and set aside.

Add the onion, garlic and bacon to the pan and cook for 3–4 minutes until the onion and bacon have taken on a bit of colour. Return the rabbit to the pan with the carrots and herbs. Stir it around, pour on the white wine and top up the pan with the stock. The level of the liquid should just cover the rabbit pieces. Bring to the boil, pop the lid on, and put in the oven forever — that is, until the meat is just starting to come away from the bone, about 2 1/2 hours. Serve with mashed potato (see Smash, page 218) or couscous (see Coo-coo, page 215), and roasted baby beetroots and Brussels sprouts. Serves 4

drinking

Bunny is a dry meat, therefore you'll need a bit more grog with this dish than if you were eating a normal stew. As for the type of wine — savoury shiraz or Victorian shiraz.

benouillabaisse

This is Ben's version of bouillabaisse, the fish stew from the south of France. We've customized it to suit Australian oceans and fishmongers.

buying

¹/₂ tablespoon olive oil
1 leek, white part only, finely chopped
1 garlic clove, finely chopped
pinch of saffron
1 tablespoon French vermouth, such as Noilly Prat
1 glass of white wine
375 ml (1¹/₂ cups) fish stock (homemade or use the stuff in a carton)
half a tin of Italian tomatoes (200 g/7 oz)
6 mussels, cleaned
4 prawns (shrimp), heads on but shells removed
2 different fish fillets or cutlets (1 salmon and 1 blue eye cod, for
  instance), chopped into big bite-sized pieces
coriander (cilantro) leaves, to garnish

cooking

You'll need a big saucepan, or a big flameproof casserole dish is better — better dispersal of heat. Speaking of heat, put it on medium. Pour in the olive oil. Add the leek and cook for 6 minutes, stirring it about.

Turn the heat right up. Add the garlic and the saffron and stir it about. Wait until the base of the pan starts to turn very faintly brown, then pour on the vermouth and then the wine. Scrape the bottom of the pan with a wooden spoon to remove the flavoursome brown bits. Add the stock and tomatoes, bring the mixture back to a simmer, and simmer for 10 minutes. Reduce the heat to low and add the mussels. When they start to open, add the prawns. Wait a minute, then add the fish. Turn the heat out and put the lid on. Go and have a drink for a couple of minutes, then garnish with coriander and serve. Serves 4

drinking

Make your own rosé to match this stew: take a chilled, reasonably neutral bottle of white (like unwooded semillon) and add 5–10% cheap red until the required colour and tannin lick are achieved. Yes, we're serious.

tips+tricks+tabletalk

Saffron: this needs to be cooked through the dish. It makes anything red-wine friendly because of its earthy flavour.

The fish: salmon will make for a richer and more oily finish; replace it with a firm-fleshed fish like bonito or Spanish mackerel and it'll be fishier, but more chewy and less fatty.

stuffed roasted pork loin

This recipe was first put to the test in the bushfire Christmas of 2002 when there was a 48-hour blackout in some areas — no oven and no food processor. The loin was cooked in a covered barbecue, and the olive accompaniment was pummelled in a mortar and pestle.

buying

1 kg (2 lb 4 oz) pork loin, skin on
3 garlic cloves, crushed
4 sprigs of rosemary, leaves removed and finely chopped
olive oil
160 g (1 cup) pitted green olives
2 anchovies
4 tablespoons roughly chopped flat-leaf (Italian) parsley
about 20 g (3/4 oz) Parmigiano Reggiano, roughly chopped

cooking

Preheat the oven to 240°C (475°F/Gas 8). If you purchased your pork loin from a butcher, don't get it tied up. If you bought it from the supermarket, cut the strings and lay the loin out, skin up. Score the skin with a sharp knife so that the fat will drain out, and rub salt into the skin to ensure extra crispy crackling. Turn it over.

Blend 2 of the crushed garlic cloves with the rosemary. Spread a bit of olive oil on the inside of the loin and spread the herb and garlic mixture evenly on the inside. Roll it up tightly and tie up firmly with some kitchen string. Put the loin in a baking tray and cook for 20–30 minutes, or until the crackling has become crackling. Turn the oven down to 180°C (350°F/Gas 4) and cook for another 30 minutes or so. Allow a total roasting time of about 30 minutes per 500 g (1 lb 2 oz) of pork. Leave the pork to rest in a warm place, covered with a foil dome for 10 minutes.

Meanwhile, put the remaining crushed garlic clove, olives, anchovies, parsley and cheese in a food processor and whizz to a chunky texture. Carve the pork and serve with dobs of the olive paste, Potato Dauphinois (page 208) and greens. Serves 4

drinking

It's the pork fat and crackling that move this piece of white meat into red wine territory. Fat needs tannin like flowers need the rain. Pinot noir is good but needs to be fairly solid because of the olive flavours. Cool-climate merlot or cab sav from Margaret River are good too.

stuffed chicken drumsticks

Don't be limited by what you are presented with — a drumstick can be deboned and turned into lots of different things. Deboning also changes the delicacy of the meat in quite an amazing way. Without the bone it goes from being a caveman to a sensitive new age guy. It cooks faster and more evenly, and there's the scope to fill the cavity with any flavour you like. Serve this as a main, but it's also a good dish to use as an entrée — one drumstick per person.

buying

8 chicken drumsticks
plain (all-purpose) flour, to sprinkle
4 tablespoons olive oil
2 teaspoons butter
250 ml (1 cup) dry white wine
freshly ground black pepper

for the stuffing:
zest and juice of 1 lemon
4 heaped teaspoons fresh breadcrumbs (2-day-old
    bread is best)
4 heaped teaspoons grated hard cheese, such as
    Parmigiano Reggiano, plus extra to serve
4 heaped teaspoons finely chopped mixed fresh herbs
1/2 teaspoon Dijon mustard
6 slices of ham
1 garlic clove, finely chopped
1 anchovy fillet, finely chopped

cooking

Debone the chicken drumsticks. To do this, use a sharp paring knife and cut through the skin and sinews around the bone at the knuckle end of the drumstick (the thin end). Then, using the point of the knife, make an incision around the top end of the drumstick, separating the meat from the knuckle. Push the meat from the bone using the back of a small knife or your thumb. The idea is to remove the drumstick meat inside out — like skinning a snake. Once this is done, turn the meat right way around again and form it back into its natural shape. Trim off any tendons dangling from the knuckle end.

Now mix together the ingredients for the stuffing. Stuff the inside of each drumstick with the mixture, pushing it in with your thumb. Sprinkle the drumsticks lightly with flour.

Get a big stainless-steel, heavy-based frying pan going on high heat, add the oil and butter and, when this starts to turn a nutty brown, turn the heat to low and add the drumsticks. Put the lid on askew and cook for 30 minutes. Turn the drumsticks over after 5 minutes or so, and turn them a few times during cooking, but be gentle with them. The critical step in the preparation of this dish is the low cooking heat — if your pan is too hot, all they'll do is turn themselves inside out again and spew out the stuffing.

Right at the end, add the white wine and let this bubble and reduce for a few minutes, scraping the bottom of the pan with a wooden spoon. Let the wine reduce until it makes a sauce — 3–4 minutes. Plate, drumstick (sit it on the plate on its stuffed orifice), a little bit of sauce, sprinkle of pepper and some more Parmigiano. As a main, serve with waxy spuds boiled in their jackets — pink-eyes, desirees, kipflers — and some simply boiled and refreshed green beans, celery or broccoli. Serves 4, or 8 as an entrée

149

drinking

Versatility is the game here — red or white. If serving this dish as an entrée, try marsanne, pinot grigio, or chardy from central or southern Victoria. Italian Soave or pinot gris, which is actually pinot grigio with another name, is another good foil. A stern, dry rosé would rock — either with the first course or as a main. Or go for red — try not-too-expensive pinot from Tasmania or the Mornington Peninsula.

The stuffing is also something you can play around with. Use leftover risotto or mix a bit of leftover stew juices through the stuffing. Finely chopped and lightly braised fennel, celery, carrot and garlic are also good.

Those leftover chicken bones? Smash them up a bit with the back of a cleaver; put them in a pot with a handful of dead vegetables — a rubbery carrot, a limp celery stalk, an old onion — and cover it all with water. Bring to the boil, simmer very, very gently for 30 minutes and you've got chicken stock to use in soup or risotto.

Is it not strange that salted meat, the food that kept convicts alive, should be in a fine dining chapter? Food links us directly to our subconscious and, like that phenomenon where hostages end up loving their captors, our ancestral convict past means that we have a certain reverence for corned meat.

pumped topside

buying

1.5 kg (3 lb 5 oz) corned topside or silverside
4 small onions, peeled
1 tablespoon white vinegar
12 black peppercorns
1 celery stalk, cut into four bits
1 large carrot, cut into four bits, or 4 baby carrots
2 bay leaves

cooking

Put everything in a large saucepan and cover with cold water. Bring to the boil and simmer with the lid on for about 1¹/₂ hours. The rule is about 30 minutes per 500 g (1 lb 2 oz) of meat. It is done when you can easily insert a skewer into it.

Allow the meat to rest in the liquid for 30 minutes or so, then carve and serve with the cooking vegetables arranged artistically on the plate, and cabbage and mashed potato (see Smash, page 218) as accompaniments. Serves 4

drinking

Corned meat goes very well with crap cabernet. You know, those fruity, berryish cabernets that always seem to taste as if something is missing. If you're familiar with the cooking of corned meat, you may have noticed that we left out a couple of traditional ingredients — brown sugar and cloves. This is because the berryish cabernet does the sweetening job of the brown sugar and the spicing of the cloves, and the tangy salted meat soothes the tannic aggression of the cabernet.

If you've spent a lot of money on fancy-pants red wine, one of the greatest viands to make those wines really sing is the standing rib roast. It's a cut of beef with just the right amount of fat and bone.

standing rib roast

buying

2 kg (4 lb 8 oz) standing rib roast
olive oil
freshly ground black pepper

153

cooking

First of all wind your oven right up — 220°C (425°F/Gas 7) at least. Take your standing rib roast and gently massage the muscles on either side of the bone with a mixture of olive oil and pepper. Don't salt the roast before cooking because it makes the meat bleed and dries it out.

Stand the roast proudly in a baking tray and put into the oven. Allow approximately 15 minutes per 500 g (1 lb 2 oz). That's the formula for rare beef and that's how this cut is best consumed. Oven temperatures vary so, after three-quarters of the cooking time has elapsed, poke a skewer into it. If it goes in easily and just a bit of blood comes out, it's done. Getting the timing exactly right is a matter of knowing your oven and roast intimately, but it is always better to err on the side of rare. That can be fixed, but you can't decook a roast. When you think it is done, remove from the oven and leave it to ruminate for 10 minutes or so covered with a foil dome.

Feel free to make a groovy gravy out of the juices: a bit of red wine, a dab of Vegemite, a sprinkle of flour, a splash of stock, etcetera, etcetera. Carve the rib with aplomb and serve with green vegetables and baked potatoes (see Splattered Chats, page 218). Serves 4

drinking

Shiraz without American oak is the wine. French-oaked versions from Victoria, the cooler bits of South Australia and Western Australia are all worthy. Full-on French shiraz and shiraz/grenache blends are good too — Côte Rotie and Gigondas are fantastic.

tips+tricks+tabletalk

Don't be tempted to dress the roast with fresh or dried herbs, ridiculous marinades or any other silliness. The reason this roast is so fantastic and goes so well with red wine is its unadulterated beef flavour.

This cut of beef is excellent cold — on its own or on sangers with appropriate condiments. Louis XVI of France knew this well. He had a stash of cold ribs in his escape coach. Unfortunately he was captured and guillotined before they could be consumed.

smoked trout salad

Even though smoked trout is relatively cheap it still tastes luxurious, and this little salad served as an entrée with the correct cutlery and stemware will not only go fantastically with your white wine, but also will impress your guests no end.

buying

154

1 large waxy potato, such as pink-eye, peeled and cut into batons
1 garlic clove, halved
1/2 teaspoon Dijon mustard
2 teaspoons sherry vinegar
1/2 lemon, juiced
1 small fennel bulb, chopped into strips
1 smoked trout fillet (200 g/7 oz), roughly broken into four portions
1 soft leaf lettuce (such as butter lettuce), roughly torn
1 tablespoon salted capers
about 60 ml (1/4 cup) olive oil
freshly ground black pepper

cooking

Cook the potato batons in boiling water for 8 minutes, or until al dente. Drain and cool. Rub the inside of your salad bowl with the cut side of the garlic clove — this is a good way of adding garlic to a salad without it becoming too overpowering. Add the mustard, vinegar and the lemon juice and stir it all around until combined.

Add the fennel, the smoked trout portions, the designer lettuce and the potato batons. Throw in the capers and pour over the olive oil. Mix it all around. Plate, and make it look cute with freshly ground pepper. The capers should serve as the salt seasoning. Serves 4 as an entrée

drinking

Smoked trout is a wonderful food for wine because of its combination of strong flavour and soft, fishy-fleshed texture. Good quality cool-climate chardonnay will make this simple salad taste like haute cuisine; and if you throw in a few softly boiled quail eggs, it's a great entrée with a rich Champagne: Gosset, Louis Roederer, et al.

Like most things, making pasta needs practice. It won't happen overnight, but it will happen. Once you've mastered the art, it's like riding a bicycle, and nothing impresses or infuriates friends, family, foe, fellow workers or future bedmates as much as someone making their own pasta. Whilst your guests are milling around in the kitchen with their first few drinks, nonchalantly mix and roll the dough, run it through the pasta machine, lay it out, plop on the filling, fold it over, stamp out the ravioli and drop them into the boiling water — all of this will render you either perfect, or a complete pain.

buying

185 g (1 1/2 cups) plain (all-purpose) flour
2 eggs
150–200 g (5 1/2–7 oz) soft goat's cheese
about 4 tablespoons pesto
your choice of pasta sauce, to serve
oh, and a pasta machine

A marble table or top is handy but any clean, flat surface will do. Tip the flour onto the table and make a hole in the middle of the pile. Break the eggs into the middle and, using a fork, beat these up, combining the flour from the inside edges of the hole as you go. Once you've made a mess, abandon the fork and knead the mixture with your hands. You're after a smooth, even, not-too-wet, not-too-dry dough. Wrap this in plastic wrap and let it consider life for 10 minutes. The dough is the tricky bit: you need to get the texture just right. Too dry and it crumbles and rumbles through the rollers; too wet and it sticks to everything and everyone. The resting time helps it amalgamate. Have a drink.

Unwrap the dough and break it into two pieces. Flatten out the first piece with your hands, forming it into a rough rectangle. Set the rollers of the pasta machine to their widest setting and start feeding the dough through the rollers. Once the dough is out the other side, fold it in two and repeat the process several times, changing down the roller's setting one notch each time. Within minutes you'll have a long piece of thin pasta. Repeat the process with the other chunk of dough.

Lay one length of pasta on the table. (If it is too long to be easily handled, cut it into two pieces.) Spoon on a little blob of goat's cheese atop a little blob of pesto every 4 cm (1½ inches), working on the top half of the sheet, and along its length. Fold the unblobbed side over on top of the filling, press out the air and seal the edges around each one. Now cut out the ravioli with your ravioli cutter or a sharp knife. Repeat this with the remaining length of pasta. (You can make the ravioli ahead of time, but keep them on a floured plate, and not too crowded or they will stick together.)

Cook the ravioli for 4 minutes in a large saucepan of boiling salted water and then, using a slotted spoon, transfer them to your saucepan in which rests the gently simmering sauce of your choice — tomato, Alla Bere Bere (page 16), mushroom, wild boar... This will make just under 20 ravioli, so serve four or five per person. That's enough if you're serving other courses as well, and homemade pasta is much more filling than industrial stuff. Serves 4

drinking

Earthy, dry wines suit this ravioli, but the choice of sauce can alter things somewhat. For a tomato-based sauce, go for shiraz or sangiovese — affordable Chianti is a good option. With mushroom, try a pinot noir. You could use some merlot if this was a poncy luncheon dish, or if this was a first course before some serious meat and its accompanying serious red wine.

tips+tricks+tabletalk

Do not use anything else in the dough. All you need is flour and egg. Don't believe anyone who tells you it's better with oil or salt.

The simple beauty of eating with others (or, indeed, alone) has vanished up its own napery.

gigot

This dish is basically a roast leg of lamb done the way they do it in Brittany, France. In Brittany the lamb is sometimes fed on the salt marshes — the flesh actually tastes like it has been herbed and salted. The equivalent here is saltbush lamb from the dry northern parts of South Australia. If you can get a leg of that, so much the better. But, whatever you do, make sure you ask your butcher for an unbroken shank. You will have to put it in the oven diagonally, but it looks so much classier than the sawn-off version.

buying

375 g (13 oz) packet of butterbeans (lima beans), soaked overnight
1 leg of lamb
6 garlic cloves
8 sprigs of rosemary, broken into smaller sprigs
olive oil
freshly ground black pepper
1 large onion, finely chopped
1 bunch of flat-leaf (Italian) parsley, chopped
rock salt, to serve

cooking

Put the soaked beans in a large saucepan, cover well with cold water and bring to the boil. Once boiling, cover the pan, turn off the heat and leave the beans for 1 hour. Drain. Return to the cleaned out pan, cover with fresh (unsalted) water and bring to the boil again. Simmer for 1–1 1/2 hours until soft — the cooking time will depend on how old the beans are and how keen they are to soak up the water. Don't add any salt to the water as it makes the beans tough. Drain and set aside, reserving a little of the cooking water.

Meanwhile, prepare the lamb. Preheat the oven to 200°C (400°F/Gas 6). At this point you've got two options. Greg skins the fat off the leg with a sharp knife. This is for two reasons: 1) your cholesterol and general health; and 2) so that you won't have too much lamb fat in the cooking juices, which you eventually mix with your beans. Ben leaves the lamb's leg as nature intended and drains the fat from the roasting dish before he mixes the cooked beans through. It's your decision.

So, the leg: slice 5 of the garlic cloves into medium slivers. Make incisions in the lamb with a sharp knife and insert a sliver of garlic followed by a sprig of rosemary. How much of this is up to you, but Greg, who's been cooking this for centuries, says if you put them every 5 cm (2 inches) or so you get the best results.

Rub the lamb with olive oil, sprinkle with pepper and put in an earthenware or cast-iron casserole dish and put into the hot oven. Allow 20 minutes per 500 g (1 lb 2 oz) of lamb leg. Once cooked, set aside to rest for 20 minutes.

Now prepare your drained, cooked beans. Chop up the remaining garlic clove. In a frying pan, sauté the onion and garlic in a tablespoon of olive oil until the onion becomes transparent. Then chuck in the beans. Mix this about.

Put the lamb on a carving board. Drain off some of the fat from the roasting dish, if preferred. Tip the beans into the roasting dish and mix them with the roasting juices. If the beans seem a little dry, add a bit of the reserved bean liquid to the dish. Put a small bed of beans on each plate, sprinkle with parsley and lovingly place the slices of pink lamb on top. Don't be afraid of using plenty of rock salt at this stage. Serves 4

161

drinking

There are few recipes where we would recommend aggressive young cabernet sauvignon but this is one of them. There is plenty of oomph in this dish — lamb juice, garlic and the floury, mealy beans — to counter the assault of this wine's cranky tannins. Go for some young Australian wines — cab savs from Coonawarra, Clare Valley or Victoria, and any other cabernet with weight and power.

gigot

malvern quail

Malvern quail is a pan-roasted dish — you do everything in one pan, which is handy when you're cooking multiple courses. The birds look cute and delicate on the plate, lending a degree of European sophistication to your evening. Yet it's a tricky little beast and at some stage or other your guests are going to have to eat bits of it with their fingers, thus helping to break down the stuffiness of serious suburban soirees. Quail is a special occasion food — you can't just get it anywhere; you've got to go to the market, which is good discipline for any aspiring cook and also shows your guests you've gone to some effort. This dish offers plenty of flavour, it's a really good match for red wine and it doesn't fill you up — you'll still have room for umpteen serves of cheese.

- 4 bay leaves
- 1 small orange, quartered, or 4 cumquats
- 4 quail
- 1 teaspoon unsalted butter, plus an extra knob of butter
- 1 teaspoon olive oil
- 1 teaspoon white wine vinegar or cider vinegar
- 60 ml (1/4 cup) semillon or dry neutral white wine
- a sprig of sage
- a sprig of parsley
- 1 garlic clove

cooking

If your quail seem a little pongy, or 'high', as game aficionados say, wash them and pat them dry before doing anything else to them. Insert a bay leaf and an orange quarter or a cumquat up each bird's cloaca (back passage). Tie the legs together with butcher's string.

Heat a stainless-steel saucepan on medium for a minute. Add the butter and olive oil, swish around the pan and then throw in the quail. Don't mess around with them. Let them brown on both sides in their own time, or you'll only cause the skin to stick to the pan and tear off. When they've taken some decent colour (this will take about 5 minutes), sprinkle over the vinegar, pour in the white wine and bang the lid on. Adjust to low and set the lid a little bit askew.

OK. Prepare the sage, parsley and garlic. Finely chop the sage and parsley, and paste the garlic (see tips, page 35). Mix them in a little bowl and give the kitchen a bit of a clean up.

The birds will take about 15–20 minutes. If the pan gets too dry, add 1–2 tablespoons of water. The key to this dish is to make sure that your quail are cooked gently but right through — there is nothing worse than a raw bird. When properly cooked, the quail naturally succumbs to the gentle pressure of knife and fork.

Remove the lid, turn up the heat to high, add the herbs and garlic and the extra knob of butter. Gently stir everything around until you can smell the garlic, then quickly remove the birds to warm dinner plates. Depending on how much liquid is left in the bottom of the pan, add a little bit more water and, with the pan back on the heat, scrape the brown bits off the bottom and then pour the sauce over each bird. Serve with Potato Dauphinois (page 208) and Brussels sprouts. Serves 4

drinking

We designed this dish for pinot noir. The pan-roasted bird, orange and sage flavours, the pan-roasting effect and the gentle gaminess of the bird itself make for flavours that are extremely compatible with pinot noir. If you haven't got a pinot, try a merlot, but just beware of those really oaky ones.

raunch.

recipes

raunch recipes

'There are many sorts of hunger. In the spring there are more.'

A Moveable Feast, Ernest Hemingway

It is an anthropological truth that human bonding takes place around food. From the broiled enemy in the cauldron about to be consumed by the hungry tribe, to the oysters consumed by candlelight with the one you love (or hope to), bonds are forged with fire and food.

Of course, no one thinks of it this way. You invite someone over to dinner (with no intention to eat them), you make some effort, light some candles, carefully choose the CDs, watch your manners, drink wine, talk, eat some food and, well, who knows? You never think that you're embarking on some primal rite. But you are. Sharing a table, breaking bread, eating of the same beast, it's all part of a subconscious process that breaks down barriers and helps you choose a mate.

Careful observance of each other's behaviour can tell you a lot about the person you're sharing the table with. Greg claims that you can discover more about a person by watching them eat than hearing them talk (he can pick someone's astrological sign after watching just a few mouthfuls). Unbeknownst to you, as your guest chews on your roast chook, your subconscious is determining if she/he is the mother/father of your children/pets.

168

The food is the focus of this ritual but is actually of secondary importance. As long as it's edible and looks alright, it doesn't really matter if the sauce is a tad runny or the tortellini are a weird shape — there are much more important things at stake.

But, beware. There's one very common trap that seduction dinners fall into. It's making the food too overtly R-rated. If you're dining with someone you're infatuated with — and dining with them for the very first time — there's usually enough sexual tension in the room without the food adding to the mix. A friend of ours tells a story of a first date with a girl he was serious about and an entrée of barely cooked egg and sea urchin roe. It caused much embarrassment. As he later said, 'You might have sex on your mind, but you don't want it on your plate'.

We've purposely avoided recipes that may cause that sort of embarrassment, but there is plenty here to show off your skills and provide a background to your bonding.

duck confit

This fantastic dish does two things for you. 1) It seems amazingly elaborate and tastes as tender and as moreish as imaginable. 2) It will quickly sort out whether the person who is sitting opposite you is, in a culinary and dietary sense at least, up to or round about your punching weight. Anyone who fiddles or frigs with this duck, anyone who gets pathological about the richness and wonderful fattiness of this dish, ain't Mr or Mrs Right.

170

buying

1 whole duck, anything above 2 kg (4 lb 8 oz), jointed
zest of 1 orange
1 carrot
1 celery stalk
12 juniper berries
6 cloves
a small bundle of mixed fresh herbs
3 bay leaves
20 peppercorns
1 heaped teaspoon rock salt or 2 teaspoons sea salt

cooking

This is a two-act play. Act One. Joint the duck (or get your poulterer to do this for you, but make sure he gives you the leftover carcass). You want two drumsticks, two thighs and two breasts, complete with the wing still attached. Chop the breast/wing joints in half again. Voilà, eight pieces.

You'll have a leftover carcass with a lot of fat covering the back. As with human beings, there will also be a little excess fat around the thighs. Trim off all of this fat and pop it into a small stainless-steel saucepan along with 80 ml (1/3 cup) of water. Bring this to the boil and then simmer it very, very gently for about 45 minutes. This should render you about 200 g (1 cup) of duck fat. Save this fat.

Preheat the oven to 150°C (300°F/Gas 2) Put all the duck pieces and all the other ingredients into a cast-iron casserole dish. You want one even layer. Pour over the fat. Make sure the duck is just covered in liquid — if not, top up with a little water or chicken stock (we won't tell anyone). Cook in the oven for 1 hour, then reduce the heat to 130°C (250°F/Gas 1) and cook for a further 20 minutes. Cool, then refrigerate. The confit will keep in the fridge for a couple of weeks, as long as it stays under the fat.

Act Two. The next day or night, remove the dish from the fridge and heat it up gently on the stovetop, melting the fat and thus enabling the duck pieces to be liberated. Drain off any excess fat. Now grill (broil) them skin-side up under a medium griller (broiler) for 15 minutes, or until they are heated through and the skin is crunchy. This is better executed under a griller rather than on a barbecue — duck fat and barbecue grills only mean one thing — the fire brigade. Potato salad, green salad, watercress, peas, some lentils...whatever takes your fancy. Serves 2, twice.

171

Once consumed, reheat the confit mixture, strain the fat from the vegetables and use it to fry chips, make omelettes more exotic, or bring hedonistic flavours to pan-fried scotch fillet.

drinking

The rich and opulent nature of this duck — it has been cooked in its own fat, after all — demands red wines with high levels of natural acidity: pinot or cool-climate shiraz. For the former, try Tasmania or South Island New Zealand, or Burgundy. For the latter, try Northern Rhône, southern West Australia or southern Victoria. Barbera is another red to try if you want to Latinize this Gallic dish.

figs, prosciutto and goat's cheese

Fresh, good quality ingredients can turn anyone into a celebrity chef. This entrée dish also offers two directions: cooked or raw. It all depends on the time of day, the inclination, your star sign...

buying

4 figs
60 g (2¹/₄ oz) fresh, soft goat's cheese, or goat's curd
8 thin slices of prosciutto
extra fancy olive oil
sea salt and freshly ground black pepper

cooking

Slice the figs in half lengthways, and smear on about a heaped teaspoon of goat product. Wrap a slice of prosciutto around the be-dairied fruit and arrange artistically on a plate. Drizzle with the oil and subtly sprinkle with the salt and pepper.

Or, pre-plating, secure with a little skewer and scorch them on a fearsome barbecue for 5 minutes. Plate, oil, seasoning, serve. Serves 2 as an entrée

drinking

Pinot grigio or semillon/sauvignon blanc blends are good here. The fig's ripe and enticing texture wants some counterbalancing acidity; the goat's cheese wants some wine fruitiness. Prosciutto is one of those foodstuffs that can be enjoyed with just about any alcoholic beverage. This dish is also rosé country and, if the mood suits, it's good with some faintly fruity fizz, like Prosecco.

Make sure your prosciutto is wafer-thin or it won't wrap around the fig as neatly as it should — and it will make the whole thing harder to eat.

tips+tricks+tabletalk

spatchcocked

Something that has been spatchcocked has been split down the middle, spread out, then grilled. The word, according to some sources, derives from the phrase 'to dispatch cock', meaning that the bird was killed, then split so it could be cooked in a hurry.

buying

2 quail
2 tablespoons olive oil
zest of 1 small lemon
a bunch of mixed fresh herbs — whatever is
    handy, but sage is nice — finely chopped
1 teaspoon balsamic vinegar
wedges of lemon, to serve

175

cooking

To prepare the quail, put them on a board breast-side down, then, using poultry shears or heavy-duty scissors, cut along the backbone. Turn the quail over and press down firmly on the breast to flatten the quail.

Put the oil, lemon zest, herbs and balsamic vinegar in a large bowl and marinate the birds in this mixture for 1 hour before you grill (broil) them, either in a hot chargrill pan or under a griller (broiler). If cooking them in a chargrill pan, weigh them down with a plate or smaller saucepan to ensure they are in full contact with the pan's rutted surface.

Cook them skin-side down first (or up, if you have an overhead griller). 10 minutes, turn them, then 10 more at a lower heat. Medium to low heat. Cooking time will vary a little according to the cooking apparatus employed. The key is to leave the birds well alone once you've initially placed them on the cooking surface — if you try to move them or mess about with them, you'll only tear the skin. Rest the meat in a warm spot for a few minutes. Squeeze over some lemon juice and serve. Good with couscous (see Coo-coo, page 215) or ratatouille (see Rat-up-a-tree, page 201). Serves 2

drinking

This is an excellent pinot noir food. Something from a cool climate but a warm, ripe year — you'll have to keep your ears open to vintage reports to solve this riddle — or a pinot from mainland Australia that's still more like pinot than dry red. Dolcetto (from Italy or a local one) is another quirky, cute, herbal and yet fruity red option.

weird peanut chicken curry

This recipe evolved from a thing called 'heavenly chicken'. One night whilst preparing this dish, the phone rang at the wrong time and Greg mucked it up. It had less coconut milk and a few other steps were skipped — but it was better. It soon became Greg's standby seduction dinner.

buying

1 chicken breast, cut into cork-sized pieces
2 teaspoons plain (all-purpose) flour
2 tablespoons olive oil
2 flat teaspoons ready-made red or green curry paste
30 g (1 oz) salted peanuts, crushed
4–5 tablespoons light coconut milk
a big handful of basil leaves, ripped up
boiled jasmine rice, to serve

cooking

Put the chicken into a recycled plastic bag with the flour. Mix it all about. Heat 1 tablespoon of the oil in a frying pan or wok. Fry the chicken pieces over medium heat until golden brown on the outside, but not quite cooked through.

Remove the chicken from the pan, lob in a dash more oil, fry up the curry paste for a minute or two — don't burn it. Return the chicken to the pan, add the crushed peanuts, then pour on the coconut milk a little at a time. Turn down the heat to low and simmer to reduce the coconut milk by two-thirds. Throw in the basil; mix it up. Bowls. Jasmine rice. Serves 2

drinking

The sort of whites that would suit this dish are those sexy, oily varieties such as viognier or pinot gris. For red, you're better off with something without too much tannin, such as cheap pinot or lighter merlot. Not all romance needs to be Burgundy-fuelled.

raunchlette

This recipe works best the morning after, for breakfast. When you finally wake up, put a bottle of very good bubbly on ice. Cook this omelette and take it back to bed, along with the bottle of bubbles. Eat, drink, cuddle, sleep or do what comes naturally.

buying

12 button mushrooms, finely sliced
1 tablespoon butter
5 free-range eggs, at room temperature
a large pinch of salt
plenty of freshly ground black pepper

177

cooking

Take your mushrooms and sauté them in a little of the butter until they are soft. Use a small non-stick frying pan. Set the mushrooms aside.

Break the eggs into a bowl, add 2 tablespoons of water and beat with a fork until the whites and the yolks are combined. Add the salt and pepper. Melt the remaining butter in the pan. (Be careful not to burn the butter.) When the butter has foamed, add the egg mixture. Using a wooden spoon, push the bits that set into the centre and the runny bits to the outside of the pan. When the base of the omelette is firm, put the mushrooms in and — using a spatula and all the dexterity you can muster — roll the first third into the centre and then flip that over again so that it is folded into three. Serve with toasted rye bread. Serves 2

drinking

Champagne, Champagne, Champagne. There is no other wine to serve with this. Omelettes and real French bubbly just belong to each other. Lash out.

tips+tricks+tabletalk

Advanced Champagne-and-omelette breakfasters tweak the omelette to go with the bubbly. Aged Champagnes adore this mushroom version, while fresh, non-vintage styles tend to prefer an omelette without *les champignons*.

sparrow's grass with poached egg sauce

You dip the asparagus into the egg yolk; a little bit of olive oil is drizzled around the edges; and there's a touch of pepper to spice things up. This dish is sadly romantic.

179

buying

1 teaspoon white wine vinegar
4 eggs, straight from the fridge (this helps them keep their shape better when slipped into the poaching water)
12 asparagus spears
the best extra virgin olive oil you can get
sea salt and freshly ground black pepper

cooking

Bring a large saucepan of water to the boil — this is for the asparagus. Two-thirds fill a frying pan with water and add the vinegar; bring to the boil, then turn out the heat and gently break the eggs into the water. Cover the pan and let the eggs cook for 4–5 minutes. You want the yolks to have just set, but that's all — it will be your dipping sauce. Use a slotted spoon to remove the poached eggs and place a quadruple-folded tea towel under the spoon to help absorb the water from the eggs.

While this is happening, snap the hard, woody stems off the asparagus spears and compost them. Boil the asparagus for 2–3 minutes at a rolling boil and then remove them to a sink half full of cold water. Give them a swim in there for a minute, then drain well.

Pop the eggs onto a white plate, place the spears to one side, drizzle some of the olive oil on and add a bit of salt and pepper. Eat this dish with your fingers, dipping the asparagus into the yolks. Serves 2

drinking

Asparagi have a taste reminiscent of sauvignon blanc or, to be more accurate, the other way around. The flavour compound in sauv blanc is methoxypyrazine — it's the grassy, capsicum smell. The compound in asparagus is methyl mercaptan — the grassy, capsicum smell. With the egg in this dish, try sauvignon/semillon blends.

gnocchi alla yours

Light, airy and very slightly mealy, these little balls of potato and flour are the ultimate raunch food. You make them for each other, you make them from simple ingredients, you make them with the happy expectation that everything is going to be reassuringly and blissfully happy. You make the best gnocchi when you are in love...

The potato is critical here. We buy unwashed sebagos (they're the normal garden-variety spud) and let them age in a dark, dry place for a few weeks before gnocching them. With this ageing they lose some of their waxiness and become more mealy.

It's best to buy potatoes with dirt still on them as they last longer than washed ones. (Indeed, the potato business has realized the value of dirty spuds: so, after the potato is washed, it undergoes a process called 'lipsticking', whereby the dirt is evenly re-applied. We kid you not. The food business is a weird and wonderful place.)

buying

the gnocchi:
500 g (1 lb 2 oz) old potatoes — sebago are good (see tips, page 180)
60 g (1/2 cup) plain (all-purpose) flour

the sauce:
1 tablespoon olive oil
1 rasher of bacon, finely chopped
250 g (1 cup) chopped tinned tomatoes
2 teaspoons pesto

cooking

The gnocchi. Wash the spuds and then bring them to the boil. Cook them until they're tender. Drain, peel off the skin (Ouch! Hot!), and pass them through a hand-turned food mill onto the table. Add half the flour and start working this into a dough. Add as much more flour as you need in order to bring the mixture to a dry but elastic amalgam — too much flour and that's how the little gnocchi will taste.

Break the dough up into four pieces and roll each piece out into a long snake. The snake's width should be no more than 2 cm (3/4 inch). Cut the snake up into little bits, about 2–3 cm (3/4–1 1/4 inches) long and roll these across the back of a fork in order to get that ribbed finish on each little gnocchi. Seriously, this takes no time at all. (You can make these a few hours beforehand and keep them on a floured plate until it is time to cook.)

Now get the sauce ready. Heat the oil in a large frying pan. Add the bacon and fry for a couple of minutes. Add the chopped tomatoes and bring to the boil. Reduce the heat to low and simmer uncovered for 5 minutes. Stir in the pesto.

Drop the gnocchi into a big saucepan of boiling salted water. (Cook them in four batches.) When they rise to the surface, scoop them out with a slotted spoon and drop them into your biggest frying pan, wherein will await your just-simmering tomato sauce. The gnocchi finish cooking in the sauce. Serves 2

drinking

With the bacon and pesto tomato sauce, try Italian reds, but spend a bit of dough, so to speak. Chianti. Or use some older shiraz. Lighter bodied, more affordable cabernets can also work well with this sort of sauce. The bigger and bolder the red, well, just make the sauce richer and more bacon flavoured. If you use a mushroom sauce, go for cheaper Italian products. If you make a blue cheese sauce, drink what you like — it won't matter...port, even...

gnocchi alla yours

ossobuco

ossobuco

Only ever-fashionable Milan could turn the hind leg shank of a calf into one of the world's most sophisticatedly rustic dishes.

buying

1 onion, finely chopped
1 carrot, finely chopped
2 celery stalks, finely chopped
2 garlic cloves, finely chopped
400 g (14 oz) tin of Italian tomatoes
375 ml (1¹/₂ cups) beef or chicken stock (the stuff in cartons)
40 g (¹/₃ cup) plain (all-purpose) flour
12–16 pieces of ossobuco, depending on their size (small pieces are best
    if you can get them — make sure you buy the real deal veal ossobuco)
80 ml (¹/₃ cup) olive oil
2 bay leaves
2 strips of lemon peel — the yellow surface only, none of the pith, please
250 ml (1 cup) white wine, anything dry
2 tablespoons chopped parsley, to serve

184

cooking

Preheat the oven to 150°C (300°F/Gas 2). Use a conventional oven and not a fan-forced one, if possible. Prepare all the vegies, open the tin of tomatoes and the packet of stock, then put a large flameproof casserole dish on the stove. Medium heat.

Flour the veal pieces lightly. Pour the olive oil into the casserole dish and brown the veal (in batches) lightly on both sides until golden brown. Remove and set aside. Add the onion, carrot, celery, garlic, bay leaves and lemon peel and cook for about 10 minutes, or until it's all softened.

Return the meat to the casserole, turn the heat to high and add the wine, the stock and the tomatoes. Stir with a wooden spoon and bring this to a gentle bubble. As soon as it starts to boil, turn off the heat, pop on the lid and cook in the bottom of the oven for 1¹/₂–2 hours. Check on the meat during the last 30 minutes of cooking — you want the meat to be just coming away from the bones. Sprinkle with the parsley to serve. Good with soft polenta or Crunchy Granola Rice (page 209). Serves 2, twice

drinking

The unctuous, gelatinous nature of this food means you can break out the tannic reds: cabernet, shiraz from places like the Clare Valley in South Australia, or the Rhône, or malbec from anywhere. Barbaresco and Barolo from Italy aren't bad either.

scaloppine

Veal scaloppine comes from the leg, not from the fillet. Good Italian butchers will cut scaloppine — or even smaller *piccate* — from this leg muscle and then pound them out between two sheets of plastic wrap, giving you the thinnest and most digestible pieces of veal you can ever eat.

buying

1 teaspoon olive oil
25 g (1 oz) unsalted butter
4 pieces of veal scaloppine
1 tablespoon plain (all-purpose) flour, sprinkled on a small plate
1/2 lemon
sea salt and freshly ground black pepper

cooking

Line your ingredients up along the bench, near the stove, in this order: oil, butter, veal, flour, lemon. Right. Get a large frying pan on the heat — high. Add to it the oil and the butter; when this begins to turn a light shade of brown, quickly flop the scaloppine in the flour — both sides — and drop them into the hot pan.

Now reduce the heat to medium. Cook the scaloppine on one side for 2 minutes, then turn over and give it 1 minute more. You may need to do this in batches. If so, rest the cooked pieces on a warm plate next to the pan. Once they are all done, return the veal to the pan to warm them through, increase the heat to high, squeeze over the lemon juice and serve. Salt and pepper and some sort of salad, maybe even a vegetable one. Serves 2

drinking

Dry, dusty merlot is good stuff here, or a blended red, such as cabernet/merlot/cabernet franc. Some of the more experimental, textural and savoury reds from Australia can offer pleasure, too: sangiovese, tempranillo and petit verdot.

tips+tricks+tabletalk

Of course, this being a pan dish means you can make a pan sauce. Once the scaloppine are initially cooked, add wine, mustard, marsala or chicken stock to the pan. Reduce this to a sauce and pour over the plated scaloppine.

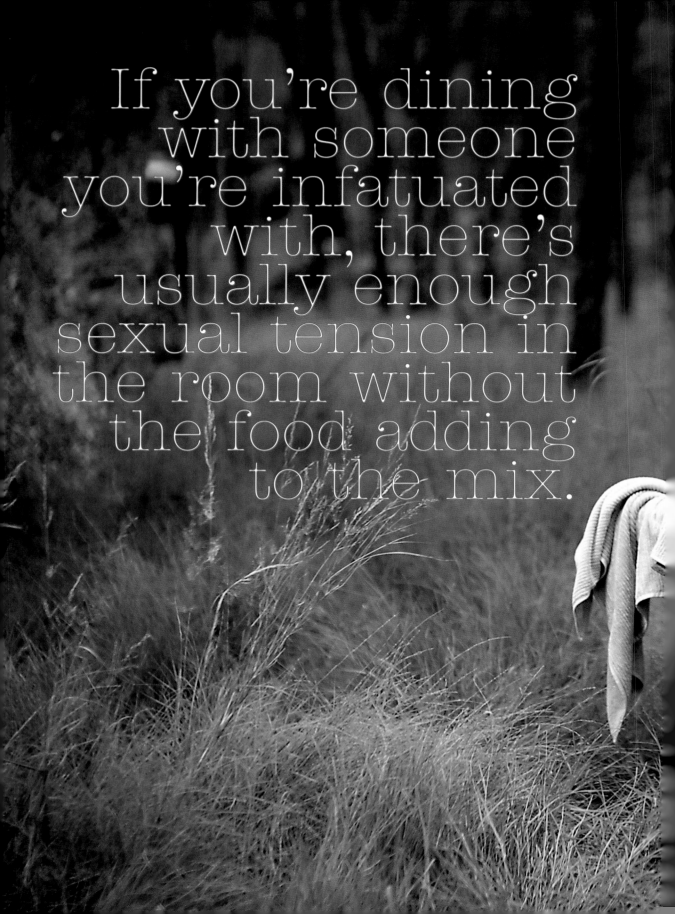
If you're dining with someone you're infatuated with, there's usually enough sexual tension in the room without the food adding to the mix.

glam snapper

Take a hot night, a hot date, a very attractive snapper dressed in foil, a bottle of wine — things are bound to happen. Whole fish in foil is raunchy food.

buying

188

1 red chilli, deseeded
2 garlic cloves
a small thumb of ginger, peeled
1 small onion
2 Roma (plum) tomatoes
a small handful of dry roasted cashews
1 tablespoon chopped coriander (cilantro) leaves
1 whole snapper (or a bream), about 500 g (1 lb 2 oz)
1 tablespoon tamarind concentrate
a drizzle of olive oil

cooking

Preheat the oven to 200°C (400°F/Gas 6). Put the chilli, garlic, ginger and onion in a food processor and whizz. Then add the tomatoes, cashews and coriander and give it another burst. Set the mixture aside.

Now to the snapper. Make sure every single scale has been removed from your fish — there's nothing worse than hitting a scale midsentence. Cut some slashes in the fish in whatever pattern you like. This allows the fish to cook evenly and all the spices to get into the flesh. Spread the tamarind all over the snapper like you're applying factor 15 to a red-headed baby at the beach.

Roll out enough aluminium foil to make a parcel for the fish. (Do this twice because you want a double layer of foil.) Smear some oil on the foil, spread half the whizzed mixture on, then lay the snapper on top of that. Now the rest of the whizzed mixture on top of the fish and a little bit of it inside the fish's cavity, too. Cook on a rack in the oven for about 20 minutes, or until the fish flakes. Serve with jasmine rice or couscous (see Coo-coo, page 215). Serves 2

drinking

With glam snapper you can't go past a good pinot grigio. It's quite a sensual wine with flavours of pears and a salty minerality.

cloaca chicken

For those who aren't familiar with poultry nomenclature, a cloaca is the correct name for a chook's bum, and this dish is so-called because a lot of garlic gets shoved up there. It's in this chapter because there is something primitively sensual about digging into a succulent, juicy roast chook with your bare hands.

buying

1 small whole chook — free range is better
1 bulb of garlic
2 celery stalks, roughly chopped
assorted fresh herbs, such as thyme, oregano, sage or parsley
olive oil
sea salt and freshly ground black pepper
crusty Italian bread, to serve

191

cooking

Preheat the oven to 200°C (400°F/Gas 6). (The secret to cooking good roast chook is a hot oven, so if you've got an old gas-powered oven that doesn't heat up past 120°C, forget it. Fan-forced electric going flat out is best.) Wash your chook in cold water and pat it dry with a paper towel. Separate the garlic bulb into cloves and put two-thirds of them up the cloaca of your chook. Fill the rest of the cavity with celery and sprigs of fresh herbs. Rub the chook with olive oil, then salt and pepper.

Put the chook breast-side up in an earthenware cooking dish (or a roasting tray) and put it in the oven for 15–20 minutes, or until the breast starts to brown. Turn the chook over so the breast does the rest of its cooking in the liquid that comes out of the bird. Cook for as long as it takes to make the skin brown and crispy. The rule is to allow about 25 minutes cooking time for every 500 g (1 lb 2 oz) of bird. Add the remaining garlic cloves to the roasting dish for the last 20 minutes of cooking time. Rest for a few minutes. Bring the whole chook to the table. Spread the garlic that's been cooking in the chook juices on bits of crusty Italian bread for added aphrodisiacal power. Serve with Bundle Hill Chips (page 203). Serves 2, with leftovers

drinking

Perhaps no food goes better with fragrant shiraz than Cloaca Chicken. The lip-smacking blend of garlic and roast chook fat, and the cleansing spicy, earthy, savoury shiraz is truly marvellous. Choose cooler climate South Australian, Victorian or Western Australian ones. Even cheapish Côtes du Rhône is good.

tips+tricks+tabletalk

The rice used for risotto must be a risotto rice, such as arborio. This type of rice releases more starch than ordinary rice, and makes for a more unctuous and flavoursome finished product.

What's raunchy about risotto? It's all in the preparation. That stodgy, pre-made and unloved faux risotto that so dominates café land is morally wrong — and unromantic. Risotto that someone has made for you, in your presence, in real time, as they talk to you about your day/the weather/your new hairdo/ or the way that arborio rice absorbs chicken stock, is the real deal.

mushroom risotto

buying

500–750 ml (2–3 cups) chicken stock
1 tablespoon olive oil
1 rasher of bacon, rind removed, chopped into thin slices
1 leek, white part only, chopped into fine rings
1 sprig of thyme, finely chopped
1 garlic clove, pasted (see tips, page 35)
220 g (1 cup) arborio rice
10 button mushrooms, halved and thinly sliced
125 ml (1/2 cup) white wine
25 g (1 oz) unsalted butter
grated Parmigiano Reggiano, to serve

cooking

Put the chicken stock in a saucepan and bring to a simmer. Put the lid on and keep at a simmer. Put the olive oil into a heavy-based saucepan or cast-iron casserole dish. Get the oil really hot, add the bacon and brown the life out of it. Reduce the heat to medium and add the leek, chopped thyme and garlic. Stir it all around. Then add the rice and two-thirds of the chopped mushrooms. Stir all that through and scrape all the burnt bits off the bottom of the pan. The idea is to brown the grains of rice before you add any liquid.

Now reduce the heat to low and add the wine, once again stirring and scraping. Once the wine has been absorbed, pour on about 250 ml (1 cup) of the simmering chicken stock, continuing to stir. Once all that stock is absorbed, pour on another cup. Then add extra stock, bit by bit, as needed. The last third of the mushrooms go in after you've finished adding the last bit of the stock. Keep up the occasional stirring. The key to this is that after the rice has absorbed the liquid, you add a little bit more — you don't want to swamp the rice with too much stock at any one time. And be sure to have the stock going at a gentle simmer as you ladle it into the cooking rice — this means you keep a more even temperature in the pot.

The entire performance takes about 30 minutes — or one bottle of conversational white wine. Once the rice is risotto al dente (that is, just a tiny bit chalky in the very centre of each grain), mix through the butter. Plate. Parmigiano. Table. Loved one. Serves 2

drinking

Pinot noir: cool-climate pinot; fragrant stuff that's not too heady or alcoholic. If it says 14% alcohol on the label, it is going to be a little bit too big. Then again, you can adjust this recipe to suit a bigger pinot: dried porcini mushrooms reconstituted in some warm water (and that same water going into the risotto in place of some of the stock), or some field mushrooms would do the job.

support

acts

support acts

'No! I am not Prince Hamlet, nor was meant to be;
Am an attendant lord, one that will do
To swell a progress, start a scene or two,
Advise the prince; no doubt, an easy tool,
Deferential, glad to be of use,
Politic, cautious, meticulous;
Full of high sentence, but a bit obtuse;
At times, indeed, almost ridiculous —
At times, almost, the Fool.'

The Love Song of J. Alfred Prufrock, T.S. Eliot

starches

When it comes to dinner, starch is the support band: potatoes, rice, couscous and so on. Rarely does it get top billing, but the star attraction would be a lonely, unplugged figure without it. You never see a menu that reads 'Chips!! — served with a side order of steak'. This is a pity because there are hundreds of different potatoes, which can be served in myriad ways. Indeed, Greg has theories about potatoes and their cooking which make quantum mechanics seem as simple as sealing a self-adhesive envelope. It's the same with rice. If it is so easy to cook, why is there so much crap rice in the world?

If meat, fish, chicken, venison or yak are the ying, carbos are the yang. And it's not just about how you cook it, it's what you put it with — or what carbo you use to balance your star attraction. Rice will soak up the curry's juices — perfect. But put rice with a dead-dry piece of barbecued steak and it's boring, hard work, bring-me-the-tomato-sauce-and-more-wine-now-please. Your juicy piece of fish is nice on its own but it isn't so good when it bleeds into your mashed spud. There is an art to starch.

198

salads

Salads are the plastic building blocks of the kitchen. With only a few pieces you can make something different every time. And, just as young children have known for decades, both are edible and provide very good roughage.

Salads are more than just iceberg lettuce and thousand island dressing: there are variants, there are multiple ingredients, and their composition and assembly is never the same. Give a lettuce to two different people and you will get two very different salads.

The salad you make is very much a product of your kitchen, your fridge, your mood. Indeed, in many ways, the notion of a recipe for salad is a little bit odd — you are better off mastering a few of the mechanics of salad making, playing with your own dressings and then letting your creative juices flow. Just as with a novel, everyone has a salad in them.

vegetables

Forcing kids to eat their vegies is completely the wrong way to go about it. Give them a dirty great porterhouse and they'll tuck into the broccoli just out of necessity. There is nothing fundamentally wrong with meat and three veg; the problem lies in the execution. After all, human beings are omnivores. We will eat everything with anything.

Eating vegetables is not just about folate, iron, vitamins or any nutritional fad or cleansing diet (or worse, vegetarianism); it's about balance. It's about the many different textures and flavours that vegetables afford. Indeed, when you think of it that way, a vegetarian dinner is a delicious possibility. It's only when you set out to make a meal strictly vegetarian that the food subsequently becomes evil. It is no longer food but ideology and, as we all know, ideology is inedible.

rat-up-a-tree

This is derived from ratatouille, which comes from Nice, in France. Eggplant, tomatoes, zucchini and capsicums are the ingredients. It's simple stuff. Being so simple, it's become popular; because it's popular, it's often subject to the most appalling execution and 'improvements' — sun-dried tomatoes and coriander...

buying

3 capsicums (peppers): a red one, a green one and a yellow one
125 ml (1/2 cup) olive oil
1 eggplant (aubergine)
2 zucchini (courgettes)
4 large tomatoes, chopped
2 garlic cloves, pasted (see tips, page 35)
a scant dash of red wine vinegar
sea salt

cooking

Remove the seeds and white membrane from the capsicums. Chop up the capsicums, eggplant and zucchini into small bite-sized pieces. Don't be too anal about this.

Get your wok or your non-stick pan on high heat. In a mixing bowl, toss the capsicums with 60 ml (1/4 cup) of the olive oil. Sauté them in the pan over high heat, tossing or stirring them around so they don't burn. 3 minutes later remove to a big salad bowl. Repeat this process with the eggplant and 2 tablespoons of oil, and then with the zucchini and 1 tablespoon of oil. The zucchini will only need 1 minute in the pan.

Once this is done, return everything to the pan (now on medium heat) and stir through the tomatoes and the garlic. Cook for 2 minutes, then add the wine vinegar, some sea salt, then back into the salad bowl. Serve, or let it stand for 30 minutes until cooled. Serves 4

201

tips+tricks+tabletalk

This is great as a first course, served on little bits of bread. Or with sausages or pork chops. Mix some through your next Composed Salad (page 206) or stir through some linguine for lunch.

The beauty of this salad is its simplicity — messing around with it is a form of emotional abuse. Celery's faint nuttiness makes it very red-wine friendly. If you've grilled some chicken, go for some merlot or cheap pinot.

bundle hill salad

At his house on Bundle Hill, Greg creates a salad *à la maison* that has achieved classic status. Whether it's his bizarre salad chopping technique or the leaves in his garden (they've survived the ravages of possums, wallabies and other noxious fauna) no one knows, but those who taste it never forget it.

buying

1 garlic clove

1 cos (romaine) lettuce, its three outer layers of leaves removed and composted

a couple of handfuls of assorted salad leaves — baby English spinach, rocket (arugula), mizuna — chopped into 1 cm (1/2 inch) strips

3 celery stalks (the whiter bit is best and the base of the celery is even better), thinly sliced

4 anchovy fillets, finely chopped

425 g (15 oz) tin of butterbeans (lima beans), drained

Dijon mustard

balsamic vinegar

virgin olive oil

cooking

Take a ceramic salad bowl; squash a garlic clove in the bottom of the bowl and rub the juice all around. Put the leaves in the bowl and toss them around, so they pick up some of the garlic nuances, as gourmets say. Add the celery to the bowl. Tip in the anchovies and the tin of butterbeans. Dress with a mixture of 1 part Dijon mustard, 2 parts balsamic vinegar and 3 parts virgin olive oil. Toss through the salad just before serving. Serves 4

bundle hill chips

Remarkable as it may seem, this will be one of the hardest recipes in the book to replicate. That's because it has less to do with the recipe and more to do with a very special oven. It sits on Greg's veranda on a milk crate. The seal on the door has perished, but the quality of chip that emerges from its charred and blackened insides cannot be surpassed.

buying

8 medium to large potatoes (see tips)
olive oil

cooking

Preheat the oven to 220°C (425°F/Gas 7). The classic Bundle Hill Chip has the skin on and is cut from a medium to large sized spud into 1 cm (1/2 inch) thick chips. They are placed on a flat baking tray drizzled with the barest amount of olive oil and cooked in a hot oven for about 30 minutes. They're not turned. The best chipping occurs when the chips aren't piled on top of each other. If you have to make a lot of chips, use two trays. Serves 4

tips+tricks+tabletalk

Contrary to potato orthodoxy, waxy potatoes such as desirees, King Edwards or Dutch creams work better than the classic chip potatoes such as sebagos, kennebecs or bingis.

bundle hill chips

composed salad

composed salad

With the careful addition of a few lumps of protein, this salad is one you could live on. It's good in hot weather, it's good luncheon food, and it's not a bad first course if you scale the volume down a little. Depending on the key flavours, you can Italianize it (rocket, anchovies, baby mozzarella), Français it (tuna, lentils, chervil), or go Deutsch (smoked fish, some boiled potato and a few pieces of fried speck).

buying

a clear plastic bagful (about 100 g/3½ oz) of mixed salad greens (the pick and mix type of leaves from the supermarket), or whatever your salad garden has
1 egg
16 green beans, trimmed
1 tablespoon lemon juice
1 teaspoon balsamic vinegar
1 teaspoon Dijon mustard
3 tablespoons olive oil
220 g (8 oz) tin of tuna in oil or spring water — whatever turns you on
2 tomatoes, quartered
50 g (1¾ oz) feta cheese, crumbled
200 g (7 oz) tin of lentils, drained
sea salt and freshly ground black pepper

cooking

Wash the salad greens in a sink filled with cold water. Spin the greens dry in your salad spinner. If you don't have one of these, use a tea towel. Put the egg in a small saucepan and cover with cold water. Bring to the boil, add a sprinkle of salt and boil for 1 minute. Cool in a sink of water. Crack the shell a couple of times and let the egg cool down.

Throw the green beans into the saucepan of boiling water and cook for 3 minutes. Drain and refresh in cold water. Drain.

Mix the lemon juice, balsamic vinegar and mustard together in a big stainless-steel bowl, then stir in the oil. Add the tuna, tomatoes, feta and lentils. Mix about. Peel the egg and cut into quarters. Add the beans, salad leaves and egg. Salad bowl or plates. Salt and pepper. Serves 4

spudski

Here's our variant on the Swiss spud standard, rosti. It's quite a remarkable dish in its simplicity and not as rich as the original version — it's cooked in only a bit of olive oil. It's important to buy the right spuds so the al dente potatoes retain their waxy, textural integrity.

207

buying

8 medium-sized potatoes, such as desiree, Nicola,
    Dutch creams
1 tablespoon olive oil
1 medium onion, diced
a handful of chopped parsley
sea salt and freshly ground pepper

cooking

Put the spuds in a saucepan with a generous sprinkle of salt and cover them with cold water. Lid on, high heat, bring to the boil, then reduce the heat and simmer until the spuds are al dente — not-too-cooked but not-too-crunchy. Drain them, then run cold water over them to cool them down. Once cooled, grate them.

Heat half the olive oil in a non-stick frying pan over high heat, add the onion and fry for 2 minutes. Remove the onion to a plate and add the potato to the pan and cook for 30 seconds. Mix the onion back in, throw in the parsley and flatten the mixture out with a spatula. The heat is still high. Now drop it to medium. Fry the Spudski for 10 minutes. Turn it over by placing a plate on top of the Spudski and flipping the whole thing — pan and all — over 180 degrees so the Spudski ends up on the plate.

Add the remaining oil to the frying pan, increase the heat to high and slide the turned Spudski back into the pan. Fry it vigorously for 5 minutes and then turn out onto a plate. Salt, pepper, and a range of meats. Serves 4

tips+tricks+tabletalk

This is the ideal accompaniment to a mega recovery breakfast: eggs, bacon, mushrooms, etc, but also to snags, schnitzel or barbecued pork. In fact, add a bit of bacon to the mix and it's a meal in itself.

potato dauphinois

The Dauphin was the French king's eldest son. Actually, *dauphin* means dolphin; but it was the title given to the heir to the French throne. This potato dish would be quite good with roast dolphin, which is a dry dish.

buying

8 medium to large waxy potatoes
   (about 800 g–1 kg/2 lb), such as Nicola or pink-eye
unsalted butter
sea salt and freshly ground black pepper
500 ml (2 cups) milk

cooking

Preheat the oven to 180°C (350°F/Gas 4). Butter a baking dish. Wash and peel the potatoes and slice them — 3 mm (1/8 inch) is the ideal thickness.

Now you must work quickly otherwise the spud slices will discolour. Layer them into the dish, adding a dot of butter and a tiny sprinkle of salt and a grinding of pepper at each layer — but not too much. Pour over the milk — the amount of milk needed will vary depending on the specifications of your dish. (You'll soon work out what's best.) Dot the top layer with more butter. Bake for 40 minutes. Increase the oven temperature to 200°C (400°F/Gas 6) and cook for a further 10 minutes until the potatoes are tender and the milk has been absorbed. This is great with roast lamb. Serves 4

Waxy potatoes are essential for this dish — they maintain their structural integrity during the cooking process.
Stock can replace the milk, if preferred.

crunchy granola rice

Like much haute cuisine, this recipe was invented by accident. Making fried rice whilst simultaneously barbecuing meat — the former on the stove inside and the latter on the barbie outside — often saw the timing go out the window. The barbecue gas would run out, the chicken would stubbornly refuse to cook through, so the poor old rice would have to go into a holding pattern. Hence, Crunchy Granola Rice...

209

buying

400 g (2 cups) long-grain natural or brown rice
2 teaspoons olive oil

cooking

Boil the rice in a large saucepan filled with water and two large pinches of salt. It takes about 30 minutes. When the rice is done, drain it well in a colander. (The less water in the rice and the longer it is allowed to drain in the colander, the less gluey it will be.)

Put a non-stick frying pan, with the olive oil in the bottom, on a low heat. Add the drained rice. The process is not so much frying as it is drying. That's what makes the rice crunchy. There is no real timing here, although it should take about 25–30 minutes. (Resist the temptation to keep stirring the rice — it only needs an occasional stir. It needs to sit on the bottom of the pan for a while or it won't get crunchy.) When it's crunchy enough, serve. Serves 4

Natural or brown rice is tastier than polished white rice. The reason for this is thiamine, which is the stuff found in the husks of natural rice. Not only is thiamine good for you but it also acts as a flavour enhancer. Ipso facto, Crunchy Granola Rice will make your barbied meat taste better too.

vegetable salad

Use this as a side dish to barbecued meats
or as a light luncheon in its own right.
Followed by some cheese, of course.

buying

an array of green and semi-green vegetables (about
    500 g/1 lb 2 oz): green beans, broccoli, asparagus,
    fennel, zucchini (courgette) — basically anything
    that takes your fancy — celery, Brussels sprouts,
    broad (fava) beans, spuds, cauliflower
1 teaspoon Dijon mustard
2 teaspoons lemon juice
2 teaspoons balsamic vinegar
2 tablespoons olive oil
sea salt and freshly ground black pepper
grated Parmigiano Reggiano, to serve (optional)

cooking

Bring a big saucepan of water to the boil. Now prepare your
vegies: trim and chop them, where necessary, into sizes that will
fit comfortably and elegantly into your mouth. Or your guests'
mouths. Add a sprinkle of salt to the water and add the
vegetables, group by group, depending on their required cooking
times. Such things as Brussels sprouts and potato will need to go
in first; fennel and zucchini only for the last 30 seconds of
cooking. This entire process should take less than 10 minutes.

Once the last vegetable has been cooked, quickly drain the pan and
throw all the vegetables into a sink full of iced water. You want to
stop the vegies from cooking and set their green colour. You have
to drain and refresh very quickly; don't mess about. Let the
vegetables cool off for 1–2 minutes, then drain them well.

Mix the mustard, lemon juice and balsamic in a large stainless-steel
bowl and then stir in the olive oil. Add the vegetables, salt and
pepper, mix gently about and serve immediately, otherwise the
vegetables will begin to discolour. Grated Parmigiano over the top
ponces this dish up. Serves 4

tips+tricks+tabletalk

Refreshing green vegetables in iced water is the thing to do with anything that grows above the ground. As a general rule, add above-ground vegies to boiling water and refresh before serving, to preserve their colour. Add underground vegies to cold water; bring to the boil, simmer and serve immediately. If only all cooking rules were that simple.

green bean salad

When you boil some beans and plonk them alongside a chop or chicken breast, well, one word springs to mind: uninspired. Here's one way to tart up green beans.

buying

sea salt
4 handfuls of green beans
$1/2$ teaspoon finely chopped or pasted garlic (see tips, page 35)
2 teaspoons walnut or hazelnut oil — yes, this will cost heaps

cooking

Bring a big saucepan of water to the boil and add a sprinkle of salt and the beans. Boil them vigorously for 3 minutes for firmish beans; 5 minutes if you like them completely disabled. Drain and refresh the beans in lots of icy water — use the sink and some ice cubes. 2 minutes is long enough. Drain again and throw back into the empty pan, along with the garlic and oil. Toss about over medium heat for 1 minute and serve. Serves 4

yoghurt and cucumber salad

If you like eating hot curries and drinking wine at the same time, it's a good idea to serve a cooling salad as well. It balances the curry's heat and stops you drinking a bottle of wine just to put out the fire. Although...

buying

4 small Lebanese (short) cucumbers
200 g (7 oz) tub good quality full cream natural yoghurt
1 garlic clove, pasted (see tips, page 35)
3 very thin slices of red onion, to garnish

212

cooking

Halve the cucumbers lengthways and scrape out the seeds using a teaspoon. Then dice or finely slice them. Put the yoghurt in a bowl with the garlic and a pinch of salt (unless you used salt to paste the garlic). Add the cucumber, mix it around and garnish with the onion. Serves 4

COO-COO

COO-COO Here's an easy way to make couscous. It will go as well with a simple barbecued lamb chop as it will with Moroccan lamb back straps.

buying

1 large red onion, diced
olive oil
370 g (2 cups) couscous

cooking

Fry the onion in 2 teaspoons of the oil until transparent. Put aside. Put the couscous in a large heatproof bowl and pour over 500 ml (2 cups) of boiling water. Add 2 generous pinches of salt and a slug of oil. Stir well, cover with a tea towel, and set aside while the water is absorbed. Then fluff up the grains with a fork and gently mix in the onion. Serves 4

polenta con patate This is the ultimate starch attachment to any hefty stew. Polenta is ground cornmeal. Northern Italians used to spend a day making it, but now there's instant polenta.

buying

1 medium to large potato, peeled and quartered
60 ml (1/4 cup) milk
75 g (1/2 cup) polenta
1 tablespoon butter

215

cooking

Put the potato into a saucepan, cover with cold water, sprinkle on 2 teaspoons of salt and bring to the boil. Simmer for about 20 minutes, or until very nearly tender. Drain, mash roughly and, using a wooden spoon, mix in the milk. Leave to one side.

Bring 875 ml (3 1/2 cups) of water to the boil in a large heavy-based saucepan. When on the rolling boil, whisk in the polenta. Do this slowly — you don't want the polenta to go gluggy. Turn the heat to very low and keep gently whisking. Within 30 seconds the contents of the pan will become yellow porridge, so discard the whisk and use the wooden spoon. Stir constantly for 5 minutes. Now stir in the mashed potato, adjusting the consistency of the mixture with a little bit of water if it looks too dry. (You want something that's like thick, gluey porridge.) All of this should take 15 minutes, tops. Stir in the butter and serve immediately. Serves 4

Traditionally, roasts got the Anglo/Aussie roast vegie treatment: a spud, a lump of Jap pumpkin, maybe an onion or some shrivelled-up nuked parsnip. Then the world went weird: lamb was cooked pink, beef was served with Italian weeds, pork was roasted Moroccan style, and people got creative with roasts and began to include all sorts of vegies — baby beetroot, asparagus, garlic... Maybe things will soon right themselves.

mixed roast vegetables

buying

a range of roasting vegetables — medium-sized
    potatoes, small onions, pumpkin, carrots,
    baby beetroot, parsnips, red capsicum
    (pepper), leek, asparagus, garlic cloves
80 ml (1/3 cup) olive oil
sea salt

cooking

Get your roast meat into the oven. While that's on the go, prepare your vegetables. Have a designated tray for them.

Halve the spuds and onions and chop the pumpkin into bigger-than-golf-ball-size chunks. Chop all the other vegetables into big bite-sized pieces, except the garlic cloves — leave them be. Mix the spuds, onions, pumpkin, carrots, beets and parsnips with half the olive oil and sprinkle with sea salt. Roast for 20 minutes. Toss the other, softer ingredients — capsicum, leek, asparagus and garlic cloves — in olive oil and a sprinkling of salt. Add to the tray and roast for another 20–30 minutes. Don't be afraid to temporarily remove the tray from the oven for 5 or 10 minutes if your vegetables look like they might be cooked before your roast is ready. Pop them back in to warm up just before serving. Serves 4

The potato salad is the food equivalent of the compilation tape. You know, those tapes or CDs you make of all your favourite songs so that you don't have to sift through the silly ballads to get to them. In a spud salad you combine all the good things and leave out the bad songs. This one has green beans and smoked salmon and NO mayonnaise.

salade de spud

217

buying

500 g (1 lb 2 oz) chats, desirees or pink-eyes (buy small potatoes so you
    can leave them whole, or cut them in half if large)
200 g (7 oz) green beans, stalk end trimmed
2 spring onions (scallions), finely chopped
2 tablespoons finely chopped flat-leaf (Italian) parsley
2 tablespoons finely chopped dill
60 ml (1/4 cup) good quality olive oil
juice of 1 lemon
100 g (3 1/2 oz) smoked salmon, torn into pieces
12 plump capers
rock salt and freshly ground black pepper

cooking

Put the spuds on the boil and do them al dente. There is a vast difference between a raw spud and an al dente spud. An al dente spud — where the teeth have to do a little work — is what this salad is all about. When you boil a potato, it cooks from the outside in. Spuds have different densities and exact cooking times cannot be predicted, but the ideal potato salad potato is cooked until the centre just changes from crunchy to edible. Taste a potato or two near the end of cooking time to check this. When cooked, drain them and set aside to cool.

Put the beans into boiling water and, when just cooked, plunge them into cold water. Put the spring onions, herbs, oil and lemon juice in a bowl and mix together. Roll the spuds and drained beans through this mixture to coat them. Add the salmon and mix through with the capers. Season with salt and pepper. Serve. Serves 4

tips+tricks+tabletalk

It's thought that a bloke named Pedro de Cieza de León was the first to take the potato from Peru back to Europe in the early 16th century. In Scotland, potatoes were banned by Presbyterian ministers. They deemed the spud ungodly because it isn't mentioned in the Bible.

splattered chats

There are many ways to cook a potato — bashing them is one of the most fun.

buying

16 chat potatoes, skins on
olive oil
rock salt

cooking

Heat the oven (preferably fan-forced) up to about 250°C (500°F/ Gas 9) and put the chats on a non-stick baking tray. Cook for about 20 minutes, or until they're soft enough to squash. Take the tray out of the oven, put it on a firm surface and, using a stiff spatula, squash the chats so that they're about 2 cm (3/4 inch) high. Don't worry about the skins bursting, as that's all part of the appeal. Drizzle each potato with a little bit of oil and sprinkle with some salt. Cook for another 10 minutes or so, or until the skins are crispy and the split bits are golden. Serves 4

smash

This is a more rustic and easily achieved version of mashed potato. Any creamy, mealy spud will do.

buying

8 medium potatoes (about 900 g/2 lb), such as patrone, kipfler, desiree, Dutch creams, washed but not peeled
1 teaspoon sea salt
1 heaped teaspoon unsalted butter
1 teaspoon Dijon mustard

cooking

Quarter the potatoes and put them in a saucepan. Remember, don't peel them — all the good things in potatoes are in the skin — and the bad things, like pesticides and fertilizers, too. Swings and roundabouts...

Cover with water and add 1/2 teaspoon sea salt. Bring to the boil and simmer until the spuds are al dente. Drain, then return to the pan and add the butter, mustard and remaining salt. Cover. Very low heat for 8 minutes, frequently tossing the contents about, lid held firmly in place. The spuds will smash up of their own accord this way. If they don't, give them a 5-second forking, or take to them with the back of a wooden spoon. The consistency of the mash should suit the nature of the dish you are serving them with. More stewing liquid or sauce = more mashing. Serves 4

splattered chats

rice and peas This is a good accompaniment to barbecued meat, a dryish curry or a roasted chicken.

buying

400 g (2 cups) basmati rice
1 large red onion, diced
1–2 teaspoons olive oil
230 g (1 1/2 cups) frozen peas

cooking

Cook the rice in 2 litres (8 cups) of salted water and drain well. The longer the rice has drained the better, and rice cooked yesterday is best.

Fry the onion in olive oil until transparent in a large non-stick pan. Add the rice. Cook, uncovered, over a low heat until the rice has gone a bit crunchy — about 15 minutes. Steam the peas briefly in a little water until tender, drain and add to the rice. Mix through and serve. Serves 4

pea mash Some food is best eaten while lying in a bed, and some food is best served lying on a bed. That's what pea mash is for — it's a pea-and-onion-flavoured bed on which your fillet of salmon or lamb chop can recline.

buying

1 large red onion, finely diced
1 tablespoon olive oil
310 g (2 cups) frozen green peas
a knob of butter
freshly ground black pepper

cooking

Gently fry the onion in the olive oil until it is transparent and soft. Meanwhile, steam or boil the peas until tender. Drain, combine the two and mash them up to a workable consistency with a knob of butter and a couple of grinds of pepper. Serves 4

orange and fennel salad

When the meat course is a little large; when you've been doing lunch, dinner, lunch, dinner; when you're over food but need something healthful to help you consume a bottle of wine, this is it.

buying

2 oranges
1 fennel bulb
2 handfuls of rocket (arugula)
sea salt

dressing:
1/2 teaspoon Dijon mustard
1/2 teaspoon lemon juice
1/2 teaspoon balsamic vinegar
2 teaspoons olive oil

cooking

Cut a thin slice off the top and bottom of the oranges. Sit the oranges on the work surface and carefully slice off the skin and white pith. Slice the oranges into rounds 3 mm (1/8 inch) thick. Or you can cut the segments out from between each layer of pith.

Cut off and set aside the feathery fronds from the fennel bulb. Remove the outer two leaves of the fennel bulb and compost them. Slice the bulb into very thin rounds.

Mix the dressing in the order listed, whisking everything before the addition of the oil. Then whisk again. Assemble the oranges, fennel and rocket in a salad bowl, drizzle over the dressing and garnish with some of the delicate green fronds from the top of the fennel. A fair bit of sea salt sprinkled over this salad isn't a bad idea, either. Serves 4

tips+tricks+tabletalk

This is great with fish. Fish and fennel are good friends. Both start with 'f'.

sweet and

sticky

sweet and sticky

'They surfeited with honey, and began
To loathe the taste of sweetness, whereof a little
More than a little is by much too much.'

I Henry IV, Act iii, scene 2, line 71, William Shakespeare

Shakespeare — a great dessert cook in his own right — knew his stuff when it came to the lolly course. But clever and incisive as he was with pen and pastry, he missed an opportunity in blending the two crafts — the sweet tooth as a means of characterization. For reactions to sugar — in both food and wine — say as much about a person as astrology or a mobile phone ring tone. Next time you find yourself in a restaurant, observe your dinner companion. Does their gaze naturally fall on the desserts listed on the blackboard? Do they skip the entrée? And as they're eating, do they seem to be saving up for something? These are the telltale signs of a sweet tooth.

Males and females exhibit the sweet tooth in different ways but, hormonal rhythms notwithstanding, there are a few things that we have observed about the sweet tooth personality. In Shakespearean terms they tend to be like Mercutio, from *R & J*. Nice to be around, they're glass-half-full people. If you dig around you'll find some parental problems, a tendency to try and look on the bright side of things when there is no bright side, and a rather fragile constitution. They're happy-go-lucky people but notoriously bad judges of character.

The non-sweet tooth on the other hand (let's call him/her the salt tooth) is almost as easy to spot. If you ask for sugar in your tea they won't be able to find the sugar bowl. When you're drinking your tea there will be no accompanying sweetmeats offered, and if you put six sugars in your tea you'll very likely receive a lecture about diabetes and dental hygiene. Bossy, tyrannical and self-righteous, the salt tooth is more like Cassius, from *Julius Caesar*, the lean and hungry type.

We have to admit (you've probably guessed already) that we're both more like Cassius than Mercutio — at least when it comes to dessert. Full-on wine drinkers tend to be. It's because most desserts make wine — even dessert wines — taste terrible. So if you want to eat dessert you have to stop drinking. This is not an option.

To rectify this, we've spent long hours in the kitchen coming up with recipes that will suit an array of dessert wines available to the twenty-first-century drinker. Herein you'll find a dessert to interest all the Hamlets, Cassiuses, Mercutios and even the Macbeths of your stage — upon which they can then strut and fret their stuff.

If you were to custom-design a dessert to go with dessert wine, you wouldn't come up with anything better than this. Greg even skips his cheese course for it.

flourless orange cake

buying

2 navel oranges
6 eggs
250 g (9 oz) caster (superfine) sugar
250 g (9 oz) blanched almonds
1 teaspoon baking powder

227

cooking

Simmer the oranges whole and with their skins on until they're soft, about 1–1^1/$_2$ hours. Allow to cool slightly, then roughly cut into pieces (skin and all) and remove any pips. Grease a 24 cm (9 ^{1}/$_2$ inch) springform cake tin and line with baking paper.

Preheat the oven to 180°C (350°F/Gas 4). Put the eggs and sugar in a large bowl and, using electric beaters, whisk for about 5 minutes until thick and pale. Put the almonds in a food processor and whizz until they're finely ground, then add the oranges and the baking powder and whizz until smooth. Fold that mixture into the beaten eggs and sugar and pour into the springform tin. Bake for 1 hour. Serve with ice cream, cold whipped cream or even egg custard. Serves 6–8

drinking

When white grapes such as riesling and semillon are left on the vine long into autumn, they often grow a mould called *botrytis cinerea*. This makes the grapes look pretty unappetizing, but it dehydrates them, making for sticky unctuous juice that — because of the botrytis — acquires marmaladey, orange, cumquat and dried apricot flavours. As we said, this dessert is the ideal vehicle for imbibing stickies.

tips+tricks+tabletalk

Quality oranges are critical to this dish. A tasteless orange means tasteless dessert. Navels with their thicker, zestier skins give better results than thinner-skinned Valencias. Blood oranges can also be used to flavoursome and dramatic effect.

slimebag's chocolate cake

Once known as 'lover's chocolate cake', this dessert acquired its rather unattractive name because of its role as an unrepentant seduction dessert. It also goes rather well with fortified sweet wine.

buying

90 g (¹/3 cup) pitted prunes, chopped
60 ml (¹/4 cup) Drambuie
3 eggs, separated
145 g (²/3 cup) caster (superfine) sugar
200 g (7 oz) chopped dark chocolate
125 g (4¹/2 oz) unsalted butter, softened
90 g (³/4 cup) plain (all-purpose) flour
90 g (³/4 cup) roughly chopped pecans
icing (confectioners') sugar, to serve

cooking

Soak the prunes in the Drambuie for 2 hours. Butter a 20 cm (8 inch) cake tin.

Preheat the oven to 200°C (400°F/Gas 6). Beat the egg yolks with half of the caster sugar until pale. Set aside. Melt the chopped chocolate in a heatproof bowl over a small saucepan of simmering water, making sure the bowl doesn't touch the water. Whisk in the butter. Off the heat, fold in the egg and sugar mixture. Then fold in the flour, nuts, prunes and the Drambuie.

Beat the egg whites with a pinch of salt until soft peaks form. Gradually add the remaining sugar and beat until firm and glossy peaks form. Fold into the chocolate mixture. Pour into the tin and bake in the oven for 25 minutes. Dust with icing sugar and serve. Serves 6–8

drinking

This chocolate dessert makes a few conciliatory moves towards wine because of the Drambuie and the pecans. The wines that go with it tend to be thick and treacly. Really intense Rutherglen liqueur muscat is the best choice, and tarry sherries are OK too.

tips+tricks+tabletalk

Drambuie is a liqueur made from whisky. In this recipe, substituting single malt whisky and adding a little more sugar can also work well.

prune tart

This is an easy-to-whip-up but nevertheless impressive dessert. You'll often find it on the cartes of quaint little restaurants in rural France. Eggy, not too sweet, but definitively a dessert, the prune tart is custom-made to go with a wine that is really good to drink but hard to find food to drink with — demi-sec Champagne.

buying

350 g (12 oz) pitted prunes
500 ml (2 cups) milk
3 eggs
115 g (1/2 cup) caster (superfine) sugar
85 g (2/3 cup) plain (all-purpose) flour
2 tablespoons melted butter
grated zest of 1 orange

229

cooking

Put the prunes in a bowl, cover them with warm water and soak for a couple of hours.

Preheat the oven to 200°C (400°F/Gas 6). Heat the milk in a small saucepan on low heat — gently and to body temp. Combine the eggs and sugar in a large bowl and whisk. Add the flour and then the butter, milk and orange zest. Butter a deep ovenproof porcelain dish or tart plate, drain the prunes and arrange evenly on the dish. Cover with the mixture and bake for 45 minutes, or until the top is browned. Serve in slices that are just warm. Serves 6–8

drinking

Up until quite recently most Champagne was demi-sec (fairly sweet) or even doux (really sweet). Dry or 'brut' Champagne only became the global norm after the First World War. (Yes, we have odd ideas about the meaning of the word 'recently'.) Demi-sec Champagne is a really sensual drink. They do still exist but, with the stickiness of modern desserts and the savouriness of the other courses, finding a spot at the table for it is tricky. Enter the Prune Tart.

tips+tricks+tabletalk

The quality of prune is everything here. The Champagne is going to cost $60+, so paying a bit more for prunes isn't excessive.

crème caramel

This recipe is really nothing more than a baked custard with a French name, but it took over the world because it can be made en masse — and en advance.

buying

345 g (1^1/$_2$ cups) caster (superfine) sugar
250 ml (1 cup) milk
250 ml (1 cup) thick (double/heavy) cream
1 vanilla bean, split down the middle
3 whole eggs
2 egg yolks

230

cooking

Make your caramel first. Put 125 ml (^{1}/$_2$ cup) of water into a stainless-steel saucepan with 230 g (1 cup) of the caster sugar. Stir this around until the sugar has dissolved and then put it on the heat — boil until it is light brown in colour. Whatever you do, don't stir it during the boiling. While it's still hot, pour this evenly into a 20 cm (8 inch) round cake tin, making sure the side of the tin has some caramel coating too.

Right, the custard. Preheat the oven to 150°C (300°F/Gas 2). Put the milk and cream in a saucepan. Scrape the seeds out of the vanilla bean into the pan, then add the bean and heat until the mixture is just warmer than body temperature — use your finger to sort this out.

Now beat the whole eggs and egg yolks and remaining 115 g (^{1}/$_2$ cup) of caster sugar in a bowl until combined. Stir this into the milk and cream. Oh, remove the vanilla bean first. Pour through a strainer into the cake tin. Put the cake tin in a baking dish and add enough boiling water to the dish to almost come up to the top of the tin. Carefully place in the oven for 20–30 minutes. The custard is finished when you can stick the sharp end of a knife into the custard and the knife comes out clean.

Remove from the oven, leave to cool, then put into the fridge. It needs a fair bit of chilling, so best make it the morning or night before the big event. To turn the crème out, quickly invert the cake tin onto a serving plate and give the base a tap. Wait a few seconds and the little blighter will drop out. Serves 6–8

drinking

A half-bottle of Sauternes or Barsac — the French sticky and sweet wines par excellence — is the go. Serve the wine half-chilled or you won't smell or taste the weirdo marmalade complexities that can ring out in these wines. And good coffee isn't bad, either. Just a thought...

poached pears in red wine

This is like medieval health food — mulled wine, spices, pears. And it keeps well in the fridge for a few days.

buying

1 orange
375 ml (1^{1}/$_{2}$ cups) red wine
3 tablespoons sugar
2 cloves
1 cinnamon stick
1 lemon
4 pears, brown ones or Corella

cooking

Slice up the (unpeeled) orange into about six pieces and put these in a stainless-steel saucepan with the wine, sugar, cloves and cinnamon stick. Bring this to the boil and then gently simmer and stir for 3 minutes, or until the sugar has dissolved. Turn out the heat and cover the pan.

Now the pears. Chop the lemon in half. Peel the pears and, one by one, as you peel them, rub all over with some lemon — this stops them from discolouring. (Leave the stalks on the pears because these look pretty when the dish is finished.) Slice a sliver off the bottom of each pear, thus enabling them to stand on their own during cooking and service.

Put the pears upright into the wine mixture, return the heat to low and cook for up to 20 minutes, or until the pears are tender. Take them out of the saucepan and let them cool a little while you reduce the mulled wine/poaching liquid to a saucy consistency, then strain the sauce into a jug (or leave the oranges in the sauce if you prefer). Plate the pears and pour over the sauce. Serves 4

drinking

Demi-sec. Semi-sweet sparkling wine or semi-sweet red wine. Lambrusco. Or a very old and probably buggered bottle of Australian botrytised riesling. Muscat Baumes-de-Venise has enough cold-tea flavour to do the job, too. In all reality, you don't need a drink with this dish. Eat it and then go and have a port or whisky.

tips+tricks+tabletalk

Once the pears are peeled, halve them longways and cook them cut-side down in a shallow stainless-steel saucepan. This makes for a smaller but equally delicious serve. One pear then serves two.

brandied oranges

Few desserts are as easy to make, as refreshing to eat, and as tipsy-making as these brandied oranges. One of the best ways to enjoy dessert wine is to have it with food that contains more alcohol than the wine. At least it brings the night to a swift, entertaining, rowdy end.

buying

115 g (¹/₂ cup) caster (superfine) sugar
125 ml (¹/₂ cup) brandy
12 oranges

cooking

Dissolve the sugar in 60 ml (¹/4 cup) of water over a low heat. This will take only a minute or so. Let this cool. Once it's done so, add the brandy.

OK, meanwhile, the oranges. Cut a thin slice off the top and bottom of each orange. Sit it on the work surface and carefully slice off the skin and white pith. Slice the oranges into rounds 3–4 mm (¹/8 inch) thick. Plonk these in the brandy mixture, along with any orange juice that's gathering on the chopping board, and let the fruit and liquid amalgamate for 2 hours, at least. A half a day is better. A full day is too long — they fall apart and go a bit blah. Resist any desires to serve this with cream or ice cream. Serve just as it is, in a low shallow bowl. And at a temperature somewhere between room and fridge. Serves 4

233

drinking

Botrytis semillon or semillon/sauvignon blanc. Barsac with about 3 years' bottle age. 750 ml bottles of someone else's Sauternes; once again, something with some bottle age — preferably 10 years — is fantastic. Dessert riesling does not work as well. Actually, forget botrytis riesling.

poached pears in red wine

brandied oranges

friggin' pecan pie

Don't hurry this out of the oven or it will deflate, and you'll swear — hence its name. This recipe is credited to Gregory's brother-in-law, Simon, who worked as a cook in a nursing home. This one was a winner. Whether using your own teeth or not, it is quite toothsome.

buying

4 egg whites
185 g (1 cup) soft brown sugar, sifted
1 teaspoon vanilla essence
175 g (1 cup) good quality dried figs, finely chopped
100 g (1 cup) pecan nuts, finely chopped
whipped cream, to serve

cooking

Preheat the oven to 180°C (350°F/Gas 4). Grease a 26 cm (10 inch) springform cake tin. Whisk the egg whites to soft peaks and add the brown sugar and vanilla. Beat again to a firm consistency. Fold the finely chopped figs and nuts into the egg white mixture.

Pour the mixture into the tin and bake for 35–40 minutes. Don't remove the pie from the cosiness of the oven too quickly, as it has a tendency to deflate. Bring it into the world slowly by turning off the oven and leaving the door open. Serve with whipped cream. Serves 4

drinking

This is a dessert that is very kind to sweet wines. It's not too sweet and the fig and nut combination makes even the clumsiest sticky seem as graceful as Nureyev. Go for cost-effective botrytised wines made from unremarkable varieties like pedro ximinez, muscat or gewürztraminer.

tips+tricks+tabletalk

The quality of dried fig is critical to this recipe. Cheap ones from supermarkets are no good. Expensive ones from health food shops are better.

lemon tart

...or tarte au citron if you are feeding a table of mechanics... Desserts don't get much more universally admired than the lemon tart: it satisfies the lemon lovers, it feeds the sugar junky, it provides cream addicts with an excuse, and it lifts and lightens the tastebuds at the end of another arduous fine dining experience.

buying

the pastry:
250 g (2 cups) plain (all-purpose) flour
100 g (3 1/2 oz) icing (confectioners') sugar
30 g (1 oz) ground almonds
125 g (4 1/2 oz) cold unsalted butter, chopped into about 12 cubes
1 egg
1 drop of vanilla essence

the tart filling:
4 lemons
6 big eggs, 60 g (2 1/4 oz) each
230 g (1 cup) caster (superfine) sugar
250 ml (1 cup) thickened cream

cooking

The pastry. Put the flour, sugar, ground almonds and butter into a food processor and whizz it very briefly, turning the machine on and off in short, sharp bursts. Less than 30 seconds of this will give you a sort of breadcrumb mixture. OK. Add the egg, the vanilla essence and 1 tablespoon of water and whizz until the mixture has combined to form a ball of dough. Don't work it too much, and add an extra tablespoon of water if the dough won't form a ball. Form it into a disc about 5 cm (2 inches) thick, wrap in plastic wrap and put in the fridge for 1 hour. Preheat the oven to 160°C (315°F/Gas 2–3).

Gently roll out the dough, on plenty of plain flour, until it is large enough to fit a 22 cm (8³/4 inch) flan ring. Roll it out to a thickness of about 4–5 mm (¹/4 inch). Be quick and don't be too fussy about it. It'll rip a little, so patch up any holes when it's laid in the flan ring. Cover the pastry with greaseproof paper or foil and then line the base with dried beans or raw rice. Bake for 10 minutes. Remove the beans/rice and greaseproof paper and let the pastry cool. Next...

The filling. Zest the lemons on a grater — use the small grating side. Squeeze the lemons and quickly combine the zest and the juice, otherwise the zest will discolour. Whisk the eggs and sugar in another bowl until they understand each other. A light beating will do the trick. Blend in the cream, gently, and add the lemon juice and zest. A few more stirs and then pour into the pastry case. Back into the oven for 50 minutes. If the top of the tart starts to brown too much during the baking, cover it with some foil.

Once cooked, remove the outer flan ring before the tart has had a chance to cool off completely, otherwise you won't get it off. This tart will keep well in the fridge for a day or two. It's actually a little better a day old. Serves 6–8

drinking

This tart yet not-too-tart tart is the best way to drink botrytised riesling. Really good Barsac with a tiny bit of bottle age is good too. The key is to find such a wine that's not cloying, but has enough acidity to stretch out the flavours of both the wine and the tart. This acid makes you want another glass of wine and another bite of tart. Perfect.

a mere trifle

And exactly that. All you do is layer cake, jam, cake, the alcohol, berries, custard, almonds and cream on top of one another, in that order. Let this set in the fridge for an hour and then scoop out. Ben eats trifle for breakfast. With Champagne.

buying

240

1 shop-bought small (350 g/12 oz) Madeira (pound) or sponge cake, cut into 2 cm (³/4 inch) thick slices
3 tablespoons raspberry jam
250 ml (1 cup) oloroso sherry
125 ml (¹/2 cup) brandy
375 g (13 oz) punnet of strawberries
125 g (1 cup) raspberries
500 ml (2 cups) good quality shop-bought custard (or homemade — see tips)
125 g (1 cup) slivered almonds
500 ml (2 cups) thick (double/heavy) cream
2 tablespoons caster (superfine) sugar

cooking

Set a layer of cake into the bottom of a glass serving bowl. Spread the jam on top. Another layer of cake, then pour on the oloroso and brandy. Scatter half the berries into the bowl (saving the rest for the topping) and then add the custard, spreading it out with a spatula. Scatter over the almonds. Now whip the cream and sugar together with a beater until it's forming soft peaks, then spread on top of the custard/almond surface. Dot the top with the remaining berries. Fridge. 1 hour. One big scoop each into little bowls. Seconds recommended. Serves 4

drinking

Sherry: oloroso — the semi-sweet one. And cream sherry. Any Australian botrytised semillon with a few years' bottle age will be fine. And Champagne at breakfast, but sweeter things like Moët… The best wine for trifle is Muscat de Beaumes-de-Venise, a sweet, luscious white from the Rhône Valley. You can buy half bottles.

berry good berries

If you've overdone the luncheon schedule a bit this week, then such a lolly course as this one will rectify the general situation. This is also the best dessert during the summer and late-summer months, when berries are in season.

buying

A punnet of every berry you can buy: straw, logan, black, blue, rasp... how many you end up with is a good indication of how generous you're feeling today

1 heaped tablespoon caster (superfine) sugar

250 ml (1 cup) liqueur muscat or tokay, or tawny port

ice cream or cream, to serve (optional)

cooking

Wash, destem and generally investigate all the berries. If any look too over-the-hill, compost them. Throw the good berries into a large glass bowl — an ornamental or slightly ornate one. Sprinkle over the sugar and then drizzle over the fortified wine. Gently spoon everything around three times. Let them stand for 10 minutes, spoon around again, and then refrigerate until needed. 30 minutes' maceration is the bare minimum; made in the morning and eat (pronounced 'et') late that night is even better. Remove from the fridge 10 minutes before serving. Ice cream or cream is optional with these berries. It's up to you. Serves 4

243

drinking

At lunch, opt for a slightly sweet sparkling wine — one of those cuvée riche styles. At night, particularly when the weather is warm, try a slightly chilled glass of liqueur tokay or liqueur muscat, from Rutherglen in Victoria. We kid you not. Fortified wines are not just for winter.

tips+tricks+tabletalk

A few drops — about four — of balsamic vinegar can be added to this, particularly if you've gone long on strawberries. It adds that little bit of weird piquancy that has the ability to transform every dish.

Leftovers make great Champagne cocktails or can be spooned into tiny dessert pastry cases and glazed before baking.

This strange frozen dessert comes via Hobart where a certain religious sect traditionally eats it on Christmas Eve. They take it with a strong drink fermented from very ripe, almost raisined, muscat grapes.

frozen hobartian

244

buying

90 g (3 1/4 oz) pitted prunes
60 g (1/2 cup) raisins
100 g (2/3 cup) currants
50 g (1 3/4 oz) blanched almonds, chopped and toasted
60 ml (1/4 cup) brandy
1 litre (35 fl oz) container of ice cream
50 g (1 3/4 oz) chocolate-coated honeycomb, chopped

cooking

Soak the fruit and nuts overnight in the brandy.

Let the ice cream melt a bit, then mix the fruit, nuts and brandy, and the honeycomb into the ice cream, being careful to prevent all the goodies sinking to the bottom. Tip into one large mould or two small moulds. Cover and stick it in the freezer until set. Remove it from the mould by immersing the outside of the mould very briefly in hot water. If it doesn't plop out onto the plate, use a warm knife to encourage it. Serves 4

drinking

There is only one drink to consume with this dessert — liqueur muscat. The best liqueur muscats come from a little part of northeast Victoria called Rutherglen. The raisiny, toffeeish, spirity aromas of Rutherglen muscat align perfectly with the flavours of this frozen concoction.

This mixture can be tailored to taste. Brazil nuts, hazelnuts, pecans, dried apricot or figs. Anything goes....

cheese please

'A dinner which ends without cheese is like a beautiful woman with only one eye.'

The Physiology Of Taste, Jean Anthelme Brillat-Savarin

What an old French sexist was Brill-Sav. And how right. Every lunch and every dinner should conclude with at least a small sliver of cheese. Hard, soft, blue — it depends more on the climate and weather and the food that has preceded it than it does on wine. Oh no, we've painted ourselves into another corner… In our profession it is almost a sackable offence to say it, but here goes: cheese doesn't go with wine very well. There, that didn't hurt too much, did it?

Wine and cheese are billed as one of the world's classic combos — like fish and chips, pork and beans, Fred and Ginger. But they're actually more like Mick and Keef — good riffs, and even better rifts. It's a battle, but a battle we perversely seem to enjoy. Human beings don't always enjoy absolute harmony. They like a fight. Will the cheese or the wine win? If the cheese is winning, drink a bit more wine. If the wine is murdering the cheese, select a more aggressive opponent from the cheese trolley.

hard cheese — cheddar, parmigiano reggiano, pecorino

This is a wide and mostly wine-friendly cheese family. Sheep, cow or goat's milk makes no great difference to the drink you're having: if the texture is dense, the acid high and the fats firm, red wine has a role. Choose reds with enough weight to counter the acidity of the cheese, and enough acidity and alcohol to help emulsify the fats. The grape variety is less important than how the wine was made. Reds that rely on skin tannins rather than wood are always a much better cheese choice. For really sharp Cheddars and piquant pecorinos, quality vintage port and even oloroso sherry is OK.

cooked curd cheese — gruyère, jarlsberg, emmenthal

This cheese family spans everything from dead-boring supermarket Jarlsberg to full-on, pong-o-rama Gruyère. They've all got that slightly rubbery texture and a nutty flavour. Beer is often better than wine: light lagers for the boring Jarlsberg, and tangy, hoppy, bigger brews with the old-footy-sock Gruyère. If you want to drink red, it's best if it is not too heavy or powerfully flavoured. Pinot noir is good. It's worth noting that if the finish of the cheese goes on and on — like it does on a stinky Gruyère — it's best if the wine does the same.

white mould cheese — brie, camembert

These are cheeses that change flavour dramatically according to their ripeness. They're fickle, and they're some of the trickiest cheeses to match with wine. The creaminess tends to coat the mouth and seal it off from all other flavours. Beer is good because it's quite cleansing and the flavours don't clash, especially where milder cheeses are concerned. Fortified wine is also an option because that extra alcohol has the power to cut through those triple creams. Amontillado sherry is always interesting, and for well-conditioned Brie try a little liqueur muscat.

washed-rind cheese — limburger, epoisses, munster

This is the most interesting style of cheese and the most tireless combatant with wine. A washed-rind cheese will always win the cheese and wine war. Stick to standard rules of engagement. Choose wines with length and structure rather than width and overt, loud flavours — wines from cooler parts of the world. And if the wine has no hope, go for the big guns, something fortified — once again, amontillado sherry. Or just drink what you're drinking and enjoy the fight.

blue cheese — gorgonzola, stilton, roquefort

In their classic, explicit forms these are really bitey, almost biley cheeses with (especially in the case of Roquefort) a bit of a metallic clang. Fruit power and sweetness tend to counter this. There are two choices: botrytised white wines have long been recommended, but vintage port is much better. The port doesn't even have to be that old. If it's young and aggressive it will stand up to the most aggro Gorgonzola all the better. If the blue cheese you're eating is a touch — how should we say — effeminate, a quality sparkling red can be a surprisingly good drink.

soft cheese — mozzarella, curd, ricotta, soft goat's cheese

These cheeses are fresh and unaffected by mould or bacteria, so keep your wine light, fresh and not too complex — crisp, neutral-tasting whites and rosés. If the goat's cheese is a bit pongy, a soft, fruity red is a good choice. A crisp lager works with these sorts of cheeses too.

wine glossary

wine words

Austere: understated fruit qualities. Lean and mean, but in a good way.

Dusty: a dry, earthy and slightly tannic flavour effect.

Earthy: smells and tastes in red wines — soil, dirt, mud, forest floor

Flinty: minerally.

Generous: plenty of everything: fruit, acid, alcohol...

Glycerol: a by-product of fermenting grapes. There tends to be more glycerol in heavier, oilier wines.

Gruff: rough-tasting, tannic wines.

Lightweight: wines without much body or weight in your mouth.

Limey: reminiscent of limes — another good description for young riesling and semillon.

Minerality: reminiscent of minerals or rocks. It's a good thing.

Oaky: poisonous...wines with too much oak flavour or odour. American oak is vanillin flavoured; French oak more spicy.

Oxidization: air getting into a wine and ruining it; a little bit of air just before drinking can be a good thing for wine, however — it wakes it up.

Piquant: wines with enough acidity to lift the flavour of the wine.

Rustic: a nice way of saying a wine isn't made too cleanly. It can be a good thing.

Savoury: flavours in red and some whites that tend more towards grown-up than kiddie sweet.

Semi-decaying reds: an old red that's been in your cupboard for a few summers too long... It's usually stuffed.

Steely: tight flavours and austerity. Some riesling can be steely.

Tannic: gruff; the textural effect of young red wines — it's like sucking on a teabag.

Tarry: wines reminiscent of tar in either colour or aroma.

Texture: the feel, as opposed to the taste, of the wine in the mouth.

Unctuous: richly textured, oily.

Zingy: acidity that races around your mouth — think sauvignon blanc.

wines/regions/grape varieties

Barbaresco: an Italian region near Piedmont that turns the red grape nebbiolo into something truly wonderful — thin in colour but with a great, long punch of flavour.

Barbera: a great Italian red grape with acidity to burn. Sausages.

Barolo: next door to Barbaresco. Also made from the red grape nebbiolo but generally regarded as a chewier, tougher wine than Barbaresco — for strong men.

Barsac: Sauternes' neighbour — a sweet dessert wine.

Blanc de blancs: sparkling white made from chardonnay. For bored people.

Botrytis: a type of mould on grapes that concentrates flavours in dessert wines.

Cabernet franc: a leafy textural member of the cabernet family. We need more of it and less of cab sav.

Chianti: Tuscan red wine made from sangiovese; usually dry and textural.

Côte Rotie: posh Rhône Valley red style, made from shiraz and a bit of viognier (a white grape).

Demi-sec Champagne: half-sweet sparkler.

Dolcetto: fruity yet savoury red grape, which should be consumed with pasta luncheons every day of the week.

Durif: strong and scary red grape variety invented by a Dr Durif. He liked powerful wine.

Gigondas: Rhône valley red — grenache with a little shiraz and mourvèdre added. It's strong stuff.

Grenache: the second most planted grape in the world. Can make raspberry cordial wine or yummy savoury wine.

Liqueur muscat and tokay: fortified wines that excel in such places as the northeast of Victoria. Every house should have a bottle of each.

Malbec: Greg's favourite. An underplanted red grape with lots of drying tannins.

Marsanne: a Rhône white grape variety that makes a fairly dry and broad wine; an antidote to chardonnay of the pineapple juice variety.

Mataro: Also known as mourvèdre. This is a red grape variety that goes into Rhône red blends. Originally from Spain where it's called Monastrell. Tarry and full-on.

Montepulciano d'Abruzzo: a red wine from the Abruzzi region in Italy, made from montepulciano grapes. Good red for oily food.

Muscat Beaumes-de-Venise: sweet, grapey, partly fortified dessert wine from the Rhône.

Petit verdot: a red grape from Bordeaux that goes into cabernet blends. Rich and quite tannic. Promising in Australia.

Pinot grigio: the Italian version of pinot gris.

Pinot gris: weighty and glycerolly white wine; a grape related to pinot noir. A speciality of Alsace.

Pinot noir: sexy red wine; power without weight; flavour without headaches; volume without a sense of having overdone it all.

Prosecco: a cute Italian sparkling wine that is ideal at breakfast.

Rhône blends: reds are shiraz/grenache/mourvèdre; whites are marsanne and roussanne. Not bad wine styles at all.

Ribera del Duero: a place in Spain where tempranillo is great.

Rioja: a posh place in Spain where tempranillo is great, but $$$.

Roussanne: a white grape from the Rhône valley, often blended

Sangiovese: Italy's premier red grape. Cherried and dry.

Sauternes: the Bordeaux sweet dessert wine classic. In older wines, taste is reminiscent of marmalade.

Semillon: a white grape that makes fantastic wine akin to lemon juice or battery acid. An acquired taste.

Sherry: the wine region of Jerez, in southern Spain, is famed for its sherries, which include fino, amontillado, oloroso, and palo cortado. Fino is pale and dry; amontillado is a drier fino; oloroso is darker, richer and nuttier; and palo cortado is dry and nutty.

Shiraz: arguably the world's greatest red grape and adaptable to many climates. Changes flavour depending on where it's grown.

Soave: Italian white wine that looks, smells and tastes of virtually nothing; it's great.

Tempranillo: Spain's best red grape; it has the tannin of cabernet, the seductiveness of pinot and the pepper of shiraz. Yum.

Verdicchio: fruity, fresh Italian white that has a bit of complexity. God invented it for fish.

Viognier: a white grape from the Rhône; better when used in red-wine making; as a varietal it is $$$ and often too flabby.

index

Ben Canaider and Greg Duncan Powell are drinks editors for various glossy food and wine magazines such as *Vogue Entertaining & Travel* and the ABC's *delicious.* They've also written wine and beer guides together: *Drink Drank Drunk — 150 Great Wines,* and *Beer: Slabs, Stubbies and Six-packs — a tasting guide.* But they also understand that occasionally they need to eat...and drink.